*f*P

How a
Selfish Ruling Class
Is Bringing
America to the Brink
of Revolution

SHIP
of
FOOLS

TUCKER
CARLSON

FREE PRESS
New York   London   Toronto   Sydney   New Delhi

Free Press
An Imprint of Simon & Schuster, Inc.
1230 Avenue of the Americas
New York, NY 10020

First Free Press hardcover edition October 2018

FREE PRESS and colophon are trademarks of Simon & Schuster, Inc.

For information about special discounts for bulk purchases,
please contact Simon & Schuster Special Sales at 1-866-506-1949
or business@simonandschuster.com.

The Simon & Schuster Speakers Bureau can bring authors to
your live event. For more information, or to book an event,
contact the Simon & Schuster Speakers Bureau at 1-866-248-3049
or visit our website at www.simonspeakers.com.

Interior design by Lewelin Polanco

Manufactured in the United States of America

5 7 9 10 8 6

Library of Congress Cataloging-in-Publication Data
Names: Carlson, Tucker, author.
Title: Ship of fools : how a selfish ruling class is bringing America
to the brink of revolution / Tucker Carlson.
Description: First Free Press hardcover edition. |
New York, NY : Free Press, 2018.
Identifiers: LCCN 2018032028 (print) | LCCN 2018037852 (ebook) |
ISBN 9781501183683 (ebook) | ISBN 9781501183669 (hardback)
Subjects: LCSH: Elite (Social sciences)—United States. | Political
culture—United States. | Right and left (Political science)—United
States. | United States—Politics and government—2017– |
BISAC: POLITICAL SCIENCE / Political Ideologies /
Conservatism & Liberalism. | HUMOR / Topic / Political.
Classification: LCC HN90.E4 (ebook) | LCC HN90.E4 C37 2018 (print) |
DDC 305.5/2—dc23
LC record available at https://lccn.loc.gov/2018032028

ISBN 978-1-5011-8366-9
ISBN 978-1-5011-8368-3 (ebook)

For Susie

CONTENTS

INTRODUCTION

Our Ship of Fools

I magine you're a passenger on a ship. You're in the middle of the ocean, weeks from land. No matter what happens, you can't get off. This doesn't bother you because there are professional sailors in charge. They know what they're doing. The ship is steady and heading in the right direction. You're fine.

Then one day you realize that something horrible has happened. Maybe there was a mutiny overnight. Maybe the captain and first mate fell overboard. You're not sure. But it's clear the crew is in charge now and they've gone insane. They seem grandiose and aggressive, maybe drunk. They're gorging on the ship's stores with such abandon it's obvious there won't be enough food left for you. You can't tell them this because they've banned acknowledgment of physical reality. Anyone who points out the consequences of what they're doing gets keelhauled.

Most terrifying of all, the crew has become incompetent. They have no idea how to sail. They're spinning the ship's wheel like they're playing roulette and cackling like mental patients. The boat is listing, taking on water, about to sink. They're totally unaware that any of this is happening. As waves wash over the deck, they're awarding themselves majestic new titles and raising their own salaries. You look on in horror, helpless and desperate. You have nowhere to go. You're trapped on a ship of fools.

Plato imagined this scene in *The Republic*. He never mentions what happened to the ship. It would be nice to know. What was written as an allegory is starting to feel like a documentary, as generations of misrule threaten to send our country beneath the waves. The people who did it don't seem aware of what they've done. They don't want to know, and they don't want you to tell them. Facts threaten their fantasies. And so they continue as if what they're doing is working, making mistakes and reaping consequences that were predictable even to Greek philosophers thousands of years before the Internet. They're fools. The rest of us are their passengers.

———

Why did America elect Donald Trump? It seems like a question the people in charge might ask. Virtually nobody thought that Trump could become president. Trump himself had no idea. For much of the race, his critics dismissed Trump's campaign as a marketing ploy. Initially it probably was.

Yet somehow Trump won. Why? Donald Trump isn't the sort of candidate you'd vote for lightly. His voters meant it. Were they endorsing Trump as a man? His personal decency? His command of policy? His hairstyle? Did millions of Americans see his *Access Hollywood* tape and think, "Finally, a candidate who speaks for me"? Probably not.

Donald Trump was in many ways an unappealing figure. He never hid that. Voters knew it. They just concluded that the options were worse—and not just Hillary Clinton and the Democratic Party, but the Bush family and their donors and the entire Republican leadership, along with the hedge fund managers and media luminaries and corporate executives and Hollywood tastemakers and think tank geniuses and everyone else who created the world as it was in the fall of 2016: the people in charge.

Trump might be vulgar and ignorant, but he wasn't responsible for the many disasters America's leaders created. Trump didn't invade Iraq or bail out Wall Street. He didn't lower interest rates to zero, or open the borders, or sit silently by as the manufacturing sector collapsed and the middle class died. You couldn't really know what Trump might do as president, but he didn't do any of that.

There was also the possibility that Trump might listen. At times he seemed interested in what voters thought. The people in charge demonstrably weren't. Virtually none of their core beliefs had majority support from the population they governed. It was a strange arrangement for a democracy. In the end, it was unsustainable.

Trump's election wasn't about Trump. It was a throbbing middle finger in the face of America's ruling class. It was a gesture of contempt, a howl of rage, the end result of decades of selfish and unwise decisions made by selfish and unwise leaders. Happy countries don't elect Donald Trump president. Desperate ones do.

In retrospect, the lesson seemed obvious: *Ignore voters for long enough and you get Donald Trump.* Yet the people at whom the message was aimed never received it. Instead of pausing, listening, thinking, and changing, America's ruling class withdrew into a defensive crouch. Beginning on election night, they explained away their loss with theories as pat and implausible as a summer action movie:

Trump won because fake news tricked simple minded voters.

Trump won because Russian agents "hacked" the election.

Trump won because mouth-breathers in the provinces were mesmerized by his gold jet and shiny cuff links.

Trump won because he's a racist, and that's what voters secretly wanted all along.

None of these explanations withstand scrutiny. They're fables that reveal more about the people who tell them than about the 2016 election results. Yet they seemed strangely familiar to me. I covered Bill Clinton's two elections. I remember telling lies like this to myself.

If you were a conservative in 1992, Bill Clinton drove you insane. Here was a glib, inexperienced BS artist from nowhere running against an uninspiring but basically honorable incumbent and, for reasons that weren't clear, winning. Clinton was shifty and dishonest. That was obvious to conservatives. Somehow voters couldn't see it. They liked Clinton.

Conservatives believed they could win if they warned voters about the real Bill Clinton. They tried everything: Gennifer Flowers, the draft-dodging letters, Whitewater, Hillary's shady investments. All of Bill Clinton's moral failings emerged during the campaign. Clinton turned out to be every bit as sleazy as conservatives claimed. It didn't matter. He won anyway. Conservatives blamed the media.

Twenty-five years later, it's clear that conservatives were the delusional ones. Voters knew from the beginning exactly who Bill Clinton was. They knew because voters always know. In politics as in life, nothing is really hidden, only ignored. A candidate's character is transparent. Voters understood Clinton's weaknesses. They just didn't care.

The secret to Clinton's resilience was simple: he took positions that voters agreed with, on topics they cared about. At a time when many American cities were virtually uninhabitable because of high crime rates, Clinton ran against crime. In a period when a shrinking industrial economy had left millions without work, Clinton ran on jobs.

Once he got elected, Clinton seemed to forget how he'd won. He spent his first six months in office responding to the demands of his donors, a group far more affluent and ideological than his voters. Clinton's new priorities seemed to mirror those of the *New York Times* editorial page: gun control, global warming, gays in the military. His approval rating tanked. Newt Gingrich and the Republicans took over Congress in the first midterm election.

Clinton quickly learned his lesson. He scurried back to the middle and stayed there for the next six years, through scandal and impeachment. Clinton understood that as long as he stayed connected to the broad center of American public opinion, voters would overlook his personal shortcomings. It's the oldest truth of electoral politics: give people what they want, and you win. That's how democracy works.

Somehow, Bill Clinton's heirs learned nothing from the experience. They mimicked his speaking style and his slickness. Some had similar personal lives. They forgot about paying attention to the public's opinion about issues.

Meanwhile, America changed. The country went through several momentous but little-publicized transformations that made it much harder to govern. Our leaders didn't seem to notice. At exactly the moment when America needed prudent, responsive leadership, the ruling class got dumber and more insular.

The first and most profound of these changes was the decline of the middle class. A vibrant, self-sustaining bourgeoisie is the backbone of most successful nations, but it is essential to a democracy. Democracies don't work except in middle-class countries. In 2015, for the first time in its history, the United States stopped being a predominantly middle-class country.

In 1970, the year after I was born, well over 60 percent of American adults ranked as middle class. That year, middle-class wage earners took home 62 percent of all income paid nationally. By 2015, America's wealth distribution looked very different, a lot more Latin American. Middle-class households collected only 43 percent of the national income, while the share for the rich had surged from 29 percent to almost 50 percent. Fewer than half of adults lived in middle-income households. A majority of households qualified as either low-income or high-income. America was becoming a country of rich and poor, and the rich were richer than ever. People who once flew first class now took NetJets.

Over the same period in which manufacturing declined, making the middle class poorer, the finance economy boomed, making the rich wealthier than ever before. This happened over decades, but the recession of 2008 accelerated the disparities. During the crash of the housing market, more than a quarter of all household wealth in America evaporated. When the smoke cleared and the recovery began, the richest American families controlled a larger share of the economy than they did before the recession.

Over time, this trend reshaped America. What had been essentially an egalitarian country, where people from every income group save the very top and the very bottom mixed regularly, has become increasingly stratified. In 1980 it would have been unremarkable for a family in the highest tax bracket to eat regularly at McDonald's, stay in motels, and take vacations by car.

A few decades later, that is nearly impossible to imagine. There aren't many successful executives eating Big Macs at rest stops on the New Jersey Turnpike, or even many college graduates. Only hookers and truck drivers stay in motels. Most affluent people under forty have never been inside one.

The rich now reside on the other side of a rope line from everyone else. They stand in their own queues at the airport, sleep on their own restricted floors in hotels. They watch sporting events from skyboxes, while everyone else sits in the stands. They go to different schools. They eat different food. They ski on private mountains, with people very much like themselves.

Suddenly America has a new class system.

Neither party is comfortable talking about this. Traditionally, income inequality was a core Democratic concern. But the party, long the standard-bearer for the working class, has reoriented completely. The party's base has shifted to the affluent, and its priorities now mirror those of progressive professionals in Washington, New York, and Silicon Valley.

Forty years ago, Democrats would be running elections on the decline of the middle class, and winning. Now the party speaks almost exclusively about identity politics, abortion, and abstract environmental concerns like climate change.

Republicans, meanwhile, have never wanted to talk about the gap between rich and poor. The party of business rejected the very idea of income inequality, in part because it sounded like a theory concocted by French intellectuals to discredit capitalism. When pressed, Republicans tended to dismiss reports of inequality with a shrug. They assume the American economy is basically just: *Rich people have earned their wealth; the poor have earned their poverty.* If anything, conservatives pointed out, the poor in America are rich by international standards. *They have iPhones and cable TV. How poor can they really be?*

This misses the point. Prosperity is a relative measure. It doesn't matter how much brightly colored plastic crap I can buy from China. If you can buy more, you're the rich one. I'm poor by comparison.

Poverty doesn't cause instability. Envy does.

This is why grossly unequal societies tend to collapse, while egalitarian ones endure. America thrived for 250 years mostly because of its political stability. The country had no immense underclass plotting to smash the system. There was not a dominant cabal of the ultrawealthy capable of overpowering the majority. The country was fundamentally stable. On the strata of that stability its citizens built a remarkable society.

In Venezuela, the opposite happened. Venezuela used to be a prosperous country. Its middle class was large by regional standards, and well educated. The country had one of the biggest oil reserves in the world. The capital was a clean, modern city. Now there are toilet paper shortages in Caracas. Venezuela has the highest murder rate in the Western Hemisphere. Virtually everyone who can leave already has.

How did this happen? Simple: a small number of families

took control of most of the Venezuelan economy. Wealth distribution this lopsided would work under many forms of government. It doesn't work in a democracy. Voters deeply resented it. They elected a demagogic populist named Hugo Chavez to show their displeasure. Twenty years later, Venezuela is no longer a democracy at all. Its economy has all but evaporated.

America isn't Venezuela. But if wealth disparities continue to grow, why wouldn't it be?

Our political leaders ought to be concerned. Instead they work to make the country even less stable, by encouraging rapid demographic change. For decades, ever-increasing immigration has been the rule in the United States, endorsed by both political parties. In 1970, less than 5 percent of America's population were immigrants. By 2018, that number had risen to nearly 14 percent.

This is good news for the leadership of both political parties. Democrats know immigrants vote overwhelmingly for them, so mass immigration is the most effective possible electoral strategy: You don't have to convince or serve voters; you can just import them.

Republican donors want lower wages. Many of them have employees. They know immigrants from the third world will work for less, and be grateful to do it. Minimum wage seems like a pittance to most Americans, something teenagers get for a summer job, but if you've just arrived from a slum in Tegucigalpa, it's a huge improvement over what you're used to.

With the enthusiastic consent of both parties, more than 15 million illegal immigrants have been allowed to enter the United States, get jobs, and use public services in a country they are not legally allowed to live in. The people who made the policies benefited from them.

What was the effect on the country? Thanks to mass immigration, America has experienced greater demographic change in the last few decades than any other country in history has undergone during peacetime. Our elites relentlessly celebrate those changes, but their very scale destabilizes our society.

If you grew up in America, suddenly nothing looks the same. Your neighbors are different. So is the landscape and the customs and very often the languages you hear on the street. You may not recognize your own hometown. Human beings aren't wired for that. They can't digest change at this pace. It disorients them. Over time it makes even the most open-minded people jumpy and hostile and suspicious of one another. It encourages tribalism.

Again and again, we are told these changes are entirely good. Change itself is inherently virtuous, our leaders explain. Those who oppose it are bigots. We must celebrate the fact that a nation that was overwhelmingly European, Christian, and English-speaking fifty years ago has become a place with no ethnic majority, immense religious pluralism, and no universally shared culture or language. It's called diversity. It's our highest value.

In fact diversity is not a value. It's a neutral fact, inherently neither good nor bad. Lost in the mindless celebration of change is an obvious question: why should a country with no shared language, ethnicity, religion, culture, or history remain a country? Countries don't hang together simply because. They need a reason. What's ours?

It's hard to think of a more important question. Our ruling class, the people responsible for these changes, ought to be fixated on it. They ought to be staying up late looking for the glue strong enough to hold a country of 330 million people together.

They're not. Instead they act like the problem doesn't exist. Their predictions for the future are confident but faith-based: all will be well because it always has been. When confronted or pressed for details, they retreat into a familiar platitude, which they repeat like a Zen koan: *Diversity is our strength.*

But is diversity our strength? The less we have in common, the stronger we are? Is that true of families? Is it true in neighborhoods or businesses? Of course not. Then why is it true of America? Nobody knows. Nobody's even allowed to ask the question.

Instead, Americans are told to shut up and be grateful. *Immigrants are doing the jobs you won't do.* There's some truth in this, depending upon what the jobs are and what they pay. But what would happen if those jobs disappeared? One recent study concluded that 20 million low-skilled American jobs could disappear in the next twenty-five years, replaced by automation. Let's say that's half-true, and the country loses 10 million jobs in a relatively short period.

What will become of the people who currently occupy them?

Many of those workers are recent immigrants, but they won't go home. They'll still live here. How many will be successfully retrained as software engineers? Maybe some. The rest are likely to wind up angry and disenfranchised and wondering what happened to that American dream they were promised in exchange for washing our underwear. It won't take much to convince them to vote for radical populists who will make Donald Trump look restrained. Things could get volatile. The cost of having other people cut your grass is always higher than you think.

Policy makers don't seem worried about this, but voters clearly sense a threat. One of the most remarkable things about our immigration policy is how unpopular it is. Only the ruling class supports it. For more than fifty years, Gallup has polled Americans on whether they want more immigration, less immigration, or about the same amount. Not a single time has a plurality supported higher immigration levels. When Americans are asked what their preferred level of annual immigration is, they almost always want less than the current norm of about one million new legal immigrants per year.

America was radically and permanently changed, against the will of its own population, by the people who run the country. Dare to complain about that and you'll be shouted down as a bigot, as if demanding representation in a democracy were immoral. Not surprisingly, many voters have concluded that our democracy isn't real. In important ways, it's not.

Immigration is far from the only example. From Iraq to Libya to Syria to Yemen, America has embarked on repeated military adventures in the Middle East. None of these wars were waged in response to a genuine existential threat, and none were popular over time. Polls have repeatedly shown that Americans think the country is overstretched and too willing to take on global commitments. Thousands of Americans have died fighting abroad. The wars have cost more than a trillion dollars and damaged America's credibility and prestige on the world stage. Enough money has been spent on recent conflicts to retire all student loan debt in America. Yet the world is less stable than it was fifteen years ago.

Have these wars against terrorism even made America safer from terrorism? It's debatable. One of the main lessons our elites seemed to derive from 9/11 is that the best way to fight Islamic terror is to welcome huge numbers of immigrants from places known for Islamic extremism.

Pretty much every major foreign policy decision in recent years has been a disaster. Yet elite enthusiasm for nation building and pointless wars continues unabated. Our leaders still seem more committed to liberating Syrian towns from some armed group or other than to fixing rotting suburbs in Akron. Our leaders seem less interested than ever in the country they actually govern. Consider the elite response to the opioid epidemic.

From 1999 to 2016, the death rate from opioid drugs has risen more than 400 percent. Drug overdoses are killing more Americans every year than died during the entire Vietnam War. Outside the richest cities, life expectancy is falling for the first time in American history due to a combination of drug overdoses and suicides.

If you were around in the 1980s, you may remember the two big health crises of that decade: AIDS and the crack epidemic. Both of these were treated as genuine national emergencies. Billions of dollars went to AIDS research. Hollywood stars wore red ribbons, held galas, and made countless public service advertisements to convince kids to shun drugs and use condoms. Congress allocated funding for the National Institutes of Health and passed laws to get drug dealers off the streets. Some of these efforts succeeded, others didn't. But it was obvious that America's leadership regarded crack and AIDS as genuine national emergencies.

Today, opioids are killing Americans at a much faster rate than AIDS or crack, but you'd be forgiven for not noticing. It's not a crisis that has interested Washington much. There's been no effort to rein in the pharmaceutical companies that flooded communities with opioids. Nobody seems to be rethinking our current rehabilitation and treatment models for addicts, which clearly aren't working. Both the Congress and the White House seem to have run out of ideas, or even the desire to think of new ones.

In a healthy society, decades of obvious failures by elites would force a change of ideas or a change of leadership. Neither has happened. The same class of lawmakers, journalists, and business chieftains holds power, despite their dismal record. America now has not only one of the least impressive ruling classes in history, but also the least self-aware. They have no idea how bad they are.

There's a reason for that. The path to the American elite has been well marked for decades: *Perform well on standardized tests, win admission to an elite school, enter one of a handful of elite professions, settle in a handful of elite zip codes, marry a fellow elite, and reproduce.* Repeat that cycle for a couple of generations and you wind up with a ruling class so insulated from the country it rules that failure goes unnoticed. A small group of people accumulates unimaginable wealth while the rest of the country becomes a desiccated husk. Yet everything seems fine.

The meritocracy, it turns out, creates its own kind of stratification, a kind more rigid than the aristocracy it replaced. Meanwhile, the meritocratic system fails to inculcate the leadership qualities that generational rule requires. Acing the SAT doesn't make you wise. Ascending from McKinsey to Goldman Sachs doesn't confer empathy. That's unfortunate for America, because wisdom and empathy are prerequisites for effective leadership. You've got to care about the people you govern. Would you be a good parent if you despised your children? Would you be a good officer if you didn't care about the lives of your soldiers?

Our new ruling class doesn't care, not simply about American citizens, but about the future of the country itself. They view America the way a private equity firm sizes up an aging industrial conglomerate: as something outdated they can profit from. When it fails, they're gone. They've got money offshore and foreign passports at home. Our rulers have no intention of staying for the finale.

Countries can survive war and famines and disease. They cannot survive leaders who despise their own people. Increasingly our leaders work against the public's interests. They view the concerns of middle-class America as superstitious and backward. They fantasize about replacing Americans who live here, with their antiquated attitudes and seemingly intractable problems, with a new population of more pliant immigrants.

Increasingly Americans have begun to understand this, and they resent it.

Historically, rulers derive legitimacy from one of two sources: God or voters. Rulers are in charge either because they claim some higher power put them there, or because a majority of people voted for them. Both systems have been tried for centuries. Both can work. The one system that absolutely does not work and never will is ersatz democracy. If you tell people they're in charge, but then act as if they're not, you'll infuriate them. It's too dishonest. They'll go crazy.

Oligarchies posing as democracies will always be overthrown in the end.

That's the story of 2016. What's remarkable is how the ruling class responded. Donald Trump won the Republican primaries, and Republican leaders immediately began plotting to take his nomination at the convention. Trump won the general election, and elites schemed to have the results nullified by electors.

Trump assumed office, and the permanent class in Washington worked to sabotage his administration.

What message do voters take from this? All your fears are real. You may have suspected our democracy was actually an oligarchy. Now you know for sure. You can vote all you want, but voting is a charade. Your leaders don't care what you think. Shut up and obey.

You don't have to support Trump to see this as a dangerous message. Democratic government is a pressure-relief valve that keeps societies from exploding. In a democracy, frustrated citizens don't have to burn police stations or storm the Bastille; they can vote. Once they come to believe that voting is pointless, anything can happen. Wise leaders understand this. They're self-reflective and self-critical. When they lose elections, they think about why.

Maybe America's most effective government agency is the National Transportation Safety Board, which investigates plane crashes. Any time a commercial aircraft goes down, the NTSB combs the site of the crash, trying to reverse-engineer what happened. Its investigators figure out what went wrong in order to prevent it from happening again. The NTSB is so good at its job that, since 2009, there hasn't been a single fatal accident involving a domestic air carrier.

If our political and intellectual elites ran the NTSB, they'd respond to plane crashes by blaming Vladimir Putin. They'd claim the aircraft was piloted by racists, or had too many white men on board. If you dared to point out a mechanical malfunction, they'd accuse you of bigotry against part manufacturers, and then ban quality control for good measure.

After a while, you'd stop flying. It would be too dangerous.

But our leaders wouldn't notice. They'd feel satisfied and virtuous. And in any case, they fly private anyway. Their planes are safe.

The aftermath of the 2016 election is recognizable to any parent who has argued with a child. Everything's fine until the kid loses interest in what you think. Once it becomes clear the child really doesn't care about your stupid rules, you lose it and start screaming. The less control you have, the more hysterical you become.

Dying regimes are the same way. They get more repressive as they fade. As their power ebbs, rulers lash out against dissent and disobedience. Deposed Romanian dictator Nicolae Ceauşescu barked orders at his guards as they led him to the firing squad.

Our leaders understood Trump's election as a direct challenge to their power. They've been fretting about his authoritarian tendencies ever since. Because they lack self-awareness, they don't perceive this as projection. They can't see that they're actually talking about themselves.

Let's say you were an authoritarian who sought to weaken American democracy. How would you go about doing that? You'd probably start by trying to control what people say and think. If citizens dissented from the mandated orthodoxy, or dared to consider unauthorized ideas, you'd hurt them. You'd shame them on social media. You'd shout them down in public. You'd get them fired from their jobs. You'd make sure everyone was afraid to disagree with you.

After that, you'd work to disarm the population: you'd take their guns away. That way, they would be entirely dependent on you for safety, not to mention unable to resist your plans for them. Then, just to make sure you'd quelled all opposition, you'd systematically target any institution that might oppose or put brakes on your power. You'd be especially concerned about churches, the family, and independent businesses. You'd be sure to undermine and crush those, using laws and relentless propaganda.

If, despite all this, election results still didn't go your way, you'd use an unelected bureaucracy to neuter any leader you hadn't handpicked yourself. But you'd be shaken by an election like that. You'd resolve never to allow one again. To make sure of that, you'd work tirelessly to replace the old and ungrateful population with a new and more obedient one. That's what you'd do.

Sound familiar? For all of his many faults, Donald Trump isn't doing any of that. Our ruling class is.

It's probably a fruitless exercise on their part. The status quo is over. A revolution is on the way.

Hopefully it'll be the kind of low-grade revolution where everybody learns something and nobody gets hurt. But it will be wrenching either way, because revolutions always are. This used to be a placid country. It's not anymore, and won't be for a while.

What went wrong?

The disaster began when almost everyone in power joined the same team. You used to hear debates between Republicans and Democrats, liberals and conservatives, on issues that mattered to the rest of the country. That's over. Our public debates are mostly symbolic. They are sideshows designed to divert attention from the fact that those who make the essential decisions, about the economy and the government and war, have reached consensus on the fundamentals. They agree with each other. They just don't agree with the population they govern.

Left and right are no longer meaningful categories in America. The rift is between those who benefit from the status quo, and those who don't. That's rarely acknowledged in public, which is convenient for those who are benefiting. The people in charge are free to pursue policies that are disconnected from the public good but that have, not coincidentally, made them richer, more powerful, and much more self-satisfied.

But not more impressive. Our leaders are fools, unaware that they are captains of a sinking ship.

This book is about them.

ONE

The Convergence

Not so long ago, politicians didn't argue about transgender bathrooms. Economic questions dominated political campaigns: tax rates, trade, labor policy, the minimum wage—those were the issues that determined who took office and who retired. The two parties passionately disagreed on economics: conservatives championed markets, liberals found them threatening. Each side resented the other, but there was a useful balance in the debate. It's hard to go off the rails when the other half of the country is watching your every move. The worst decisions always come from unquestioned bipartisan consensus, which over time is exactly what we got from the leaders of both parties.

I watched this convergence.

I grew up in California in the 1970s, surrounded by

old-fashioned liberals, people who considered market capitalism a communicable disease. I lived in a liberal town, went to a liberal school, had liberal relatives living in my house. My aunt was a nudist who put raw honey in her hair when she sunbathed and later ran an organic mutton farm. Kids in my class smoked weed with their parents. The dominant religion in the neighborhood was astrology. Liberals were everywhere. They smelled like patchouli. They showed up late to everything. They talked incessantly about solar power, humpback whales, and the Hopi Indians. They annoyed the hell out of me.

Nobody got on my nerves more than Mrs. Raymond, my first-grade teacher. Even by the standards of 1975, Mrs. Raymond was a living parody of earth-mother liberalism. She wore long Indian-print skirts with turtlenecks and sandals and dangly beaded earrings that looked like wind chimes. She had little interest in conventional academic topics, like reading and penmanship. Her real passion was socially conscious art projects, so that's what we spent a lot of our class time doing. We made god's eyes from Popsicle sticks and yarn, in solidarity with the indigenous peoples of Mexico. We finger-painted Greenpeace slogans. We built solar ovens from aluminum foil, in protest of fossil fuels, and used them to cook lunch.

Like a lot of liberals back then, Mrs. Raymond believed that the act of eating entailed important moral choices. Lunch was never just lunch; it was a statement about your values. Mrs. Raymond talked a lot about food. Some foods were virtuous (sprouts and tofu), while others were irredeemably sinful (sugary breakfast cereals).

Nothing was more unethical than white bread, which Mrs. Raymond described as the product of ruling-class oppression.

Medieval lords could afford to have the bran milled from their grain, while the peasants made due with hearty brown loaves. But in the end the joke was on the lords. With no nutrition in their bread, they died earlier than their macrobiotic serfs.

Was any of this true? I have no idea, but it made for a memorable parable. To this day, the sight of Wonder Bread makes me anxious.

Mrs. Raymond was obviously political, but she never said so directly. Most of her statements came in the form of questions: "Why do you think the settlers did that?" "Is watering your lawn really a good idea?" Or, most commonly, "Do you think [this or that example of capitalism] seems fair?" She had the gold medal in passive aggression.

Mrs. Raymond felt pain at the thought of injustice anywhere. And from her perspective, it was everywhere. Baby seals were being clubbed. Nuclear reactors were being built. People were eating Cap'n Crunch.

One afternoon she finally snapped under the weight of it all. We filed back into class after recess to find her sitting at the front of the room looking distracted. "Please sit down," she said, "and put your heads on your desks." She turned off the lights and said nothing. For what seemed like an hour, we sat in dark silence. Were we in trouble? Had someone died? It was confusing, and kind of scary.

Then without warning Mrs. Raymond started sobbing— and not quietly, but with theatrical flamboyance, in a desperate, trying-to-catch-her-breath-between-convulsions way. I opened my eyes to look, along with everyone else in the class. She met our stares and tried to explain: "The world is so unfair!" she yelped. "You don't know that yet. But you'll find out!"

Mrs. Raymond was a sensitive plant. But she wasn't entirely wrong. As the years passed, the world proved to be every bit as unfair as she predicted, in big ways and small. Almost nothing seemed to be decided fairly, from who gets chosen for the kickball team, to who develops ALS, to who wins a spot at Harvard Business School. The wicked prosper, the decent suffer, and there's not much we can do about it. A distressingly large percentage of life is beyond our control. It's random, baked in the cake at birth, or else determined by larger forces hostile or indifferent to our interests. We rarely get what we deserve, for good or bad.

This has been true for all human history, but when I was a kid it formed the basis of the political divide. Conservatives accepted the basic unfairness of life. Liberals raged against it. As a conservative, I had contempt for the whiny mawkishness of liberals. Stop blubbering and teach us to read. That was my position. (Mrs. Raymond never did teach us; my father had to hire a tutor to get me through phonics.)

Forty years later, I still feel that way. But I also miss people like Mrs. Raymond.

In retrospect it was important to have sincere liberals around. Someone needs to fret about the excesses of capitalism. When liberals stopped doing that, the country lost a needed counterbalance. In an ecosystem, every species has a role to play, even the pests. If you succeeded in eliminating the mosquitos, birds would starve.

When the last liberal stopped sobbing about unfairness, American society became less fair.

It's hard to know exactly when this happened, though it became obvious during the tech boom of the 1990s. That's the first time I remember wondering why liberals weren't complaining about big business. Until then, whining about corporate power had been the soundtrack of the left. Businessmen were bad; the more successful, the more sinister. For one hundred years, from the Progressive era to the second Clinton administration, liberals never ceased making that point.

And then one day they stopped. I remember picking up *Newsweek* and seeing America's new corporate chieftains described as heroes. Steve Jobs, Bill Gates, the Google guys— nobody was accusing them of exploiting workers or getting too rich. Just the opposite. Liberals were celebrating their wealth and assuring us their products would liberate the world. Conservatives didn't complain. They'd always celebrated business. Suddenly both sides were aligned on the virtues of unrestrained market capitalism.

Before long, left and right were taking virtually indistinguishable positions on many economic issues, especially on wages.

Mass immigration? The Chamber of Commerce had long supported more of it. Liberals were now on board, too.

Self-driving cars? Drone delivery of packages? Trucking companies love the idea. It means they won't have to pay drivers. Lawmakers in both parties love the idea, too. It's such impressive technology. If America doesn't lead the way, someone else will.

Neither side mentions the potential effect on employment. There are more than three million professional truck drivers in the United States. Driving is the most common job in the majority of states, the biggest single employer in blue-collar America.

Technology is poised to destroy all of those jobs, and the communities they support, overnight.

Washington isn't worried. Democrats assure doubters that

those truck drivers will be just fine. They'll find something else to do, something better, with higher pay. That's almost exactly what corporate Republicans said about disappearing manufacturing jobs thirty years ago.

The difference is, thirty years ago there were prolabor Democrats to push back.

Ironically, some of the most successful players in the new economy, the ones who were going to free us from drudgery, have embraced the most retrograde labor practices.

Think migrant farmworkers have it bad? Talk to anyone who works in an Amazon fulfillment center, where every step an employee takes is tracked electronically by management; fail to account for a five-minute period and you're punished. No textile mill ever dehumanized its workers more thoroughly.

Yet when was the last time you heard a liberal criticize working conditions at Amazon? You won't. Amazon is the future. Jeff Bezos supported Hillary for president.

So did virtually all the most successful CEOs. Amazingly, liberals support them back.

The distinction between successful businessman and progressive political activist gets blurrier by the day.

———

The few sincere liberals left, the ones actually fighting corporate power, seem like bewildered relics from an earlier age. For generations, there was no more famous activist on the left than Ralph Nader. Nader became a national figure in 1965, when he published his book *Unsafe at Any Speed*. Nader accused Detroit of knowingly selling dangerous cars. The charge was basically true. General Motors responded by discontinuing the Chevrolet

Corvair. The company also tapped Nader's phones and, it later admitted, hired prostitutes to seduce him.

If life were fair, Nader would be living out his days in a socialist retirement home in Florida, greeting a parade of awe-struck liberal pilgrims. Instead, he's mostly reviled by his former admirers. His crime was daring to run for president in 2000. Democrats blamed him for Al Gore's narrow loss to George W. Bush. They never stopped blaming him. "Ralph Nader Still Refuses to Admit He Elected Bush," read a headline in *New York* magazine sixteen years after the election.

By the time Trump became president, Nader was mostly forgotten. He lived in a small apartment in Washington, writing op-eds that he posted to his own lightly trafficked website. Nader's politics never changed. He still believed that unchecked corporate power posed a threat to American democracy. By the summer of 2017, he'd turned his sights on the most powerful corporate leader of all, Jeff Bezos of Amazon.

"As Amazon spreads around the world selling everything and squeezing other businesses that use its platform," Nader wrote, "is Bezos laughing at humanity? His ultimate objective seems to preside over a mega-trillion dollar global juggernaut that is largely automated, except for that man at the top with the booming laugh who rules over the means by which we consume everything from goods, to media, to groceries."

Nader went on to attack Bezos for crushing labor unions and creating a dangerous monopoly that hurts consumers. Every point Nader made was fair. Some were indisputably true.

Nobody cared. By 2017, liberals and Jeff Bezos were playing for the same team. Bezos was now the owner of the *Washington Post*, the most aggressively anti-Trump newspaper in the United

States. To liberals, Bezos wasn't a corporate villain. He was a role model. *Slate*, the online newsletter of well-educated young progressives in New York and Washington, published stories with headlines like "The Peculiar Genius of Jeff Bezos."

Two weeks after Nader posted his worries about Amazon's effect on unions and consumers, *Slate* wrote this about Bezos: "The Amazon CEO and *Washington Post* owner showed up to an Idaho conference in a skintight T-shirt last week, displaying a set of arms most reasonable observers would classify as assault weapons."

It's hard to imagine *Slate* writing anything at all about Ralph Nader, even gushy pieces about his arms. Nader is a living rebuke to modern liberalism. Not only did he once dare to run for president without permission, but he's consistently refused to suck up to power. Modern progressives despise him for that above all.

———

The Democratic Party is now the party of the rich. Eight of America's ten most affluent counties voted for Hillary Clinton in 2016, in most cases by a large margin. In Fairfield County, Connecticut, the hedge fund capital of the world, Hillary won by nearly 20 points. In Nantucket, she won by more than 30 points. In Aspen, Hillary won by more than 45 points. In Marin County, the privileged enclave across the Golden Gate from San Francisco, Hillary Clinton's margin was greater than 50 points.

In Manhattan, by contrast, Trump won less than 10 percent of the vote. In the District of Columbia, he got 4 percent, a smaller proportion than third-party candidates and write-ins combined.

Historically, most highly paid executives voted Republican. No more. In the weeks before the 2016 election, Hillary Clinton outraised Donald Trump 20-to-1 among people on the Bloomberg Billionaires Index. A *Wall Street Journal* analysis found that hedge fund owners and employees donated a total of $27.6 million to the Hillary Clinton campaign and affiliated groups. When the category was expanded to include "similar private investment funds," the *Journal* found that seven financial firms alone donated $47.6 million to Hillary. Trump received a total of $19,000, about the price of a used pickup.

Employees of Google, Facebook, Apple, Microsoft, and Amazon donated to Hillary over Trump by a margin of 60-to-1.

George Soros was on the leading edge of this trend. Long before he became famous as one of the biggest Democratic donors in history, Soros was best known for getting rich by betting against national currencies, notably the English pound. Soros was considered such a rapacious and unethical practitioner of vulture capitalism that liberal economist Paul Krugman once accused him of intentionally trying to provoke currency crises in order to profit from them.

Krugman no longer criticizes Soros, who has gone on to spend billions on behalf of liberal candidates and policy positions around the world. It now seems normal for businessmen to finance the activist left. A generation or two ago, it would have been inconceivable. Try to imagine Dow Chemical, makers of Agent Orange, funding antiwar protests during Vietnam. Or maybe General Motors backing the UAW during the auto strike of 1946. That's what it's like. Weird, at the very least.

It's also inevitable. In 1980, Yippie icon Jerry Rubin gave up protesting capitalism to work on Wall Street. Well-educated baby boom liberals began to join the establishment in droves. By the late 1990s, they were in charge. Thanks to the rise of the finance economy, they were getting richer than any previous generation ever had. Nothing changes a person's attitude toward money like earning a lot of it. It's hard to feel rage toward the Man when you're buying a ski house in Sun Valley.

So young liberals grew up and became the establishment they once despised. That's a familiar story. What's new is that this new class felt little responsibility to those beneath them. The meritocracy convinced them that the existing order is the natural order.

Designed by well-meaning academics to make American society fairer, standardized testing transformed the attitudes of the privileged. Unlike the nineteenth-century robber barons, relatively few in the modern ruling class had ever lived among their employees. (Andrew Carnegie, by contrast, went to work in a cotton mill at thirteen.) They had little understanding of the defining role luck often plays in life. People who do the right thing often fail anyway. Human power has limits. You're not always the sum of your choices. That was hard to deny one hundred years ago, when even tycoons routinely watched their children suffocate from diphtheria.

The main reason elites no longer talk about unfairness is that they don't believe it exists. They're successful because they deserve to be: that's the message of the system they grew up in.

The flip side of believing the rich deserve it is deciding the poor do, too. This is the unspoken but core assumption of modern American elites: I went to Yale and live on ten acres in Greenwich because I worked hard and made wise choices. You're unemployed and live in an apartment in Cleveland because you didn't. The system doesn't produce equal results, yet it's still basically fair because the best people inevitably rise to the top. The affluent now believe that. It's a kind of secular Calvinism. This is not an improvement over what Mrs. Raymond was pushing. The best thing about old-fashioned liberals was how guilty they were. They felt bad about everything, and that kept them empathetic and humane. It also made them instinctively suspicious of power, which was useful. Somebody needs to be.

In March 1911, the Triangle Shirtwaist factory in lower Manhattan caught fire. Close to 150 people died, nearly half after jumping from upper floors onto the sidewalk. The fire started accidentally, when a garment worker dropped a lit cigarette into a bin of fabric cuttings, but the high death toll could have been prevented. The company's owners had padlocked interior doors to prevent theft, trapping workers in the flames. Those who made it to the exits found the tiny stairwells clogged with bodies. Scores were crushed. The few who reached the shoddily made fire escape fell to their deaths when it detached from the side of the building.

The Triangle Shirtwaist Fire was a human disaster, the deadliest fire in the history of New York at the time, but soon it became notorious around the world as a metaphor for the mistreatment of workers. Dozens of books and countless pamphlets were written about the fire. The International Ladies' Garment Workers' Union swelled to become one of the most powerful forces in organized labor. For decades, what happened at the Triangle Shirtwaist factory was a rallying cry of the progressive movement.

Fast-forward one hundred years. The ILGWU is long gone, dissolved in the 1990s. But so are the attitudes that celebrated it. Millions of people around the world still work in factories, but you don't hear much about them. What would happen if there were the equivalent of a Triangle Shirtwaist fire at, say, an iPhone factory in China? Would anyone care? Actually, we know the answer.

The phone you have in your pocket right now was likely made in China by Foxconn, a Taiwanese company that is the biggest electronics manufacturer in the world. The workers who assembled it made less than two dollars an hour. Even by Chinese standards, that's not a lot. Foxconn employees who make iPhones would have to work for months to afford one.

The work at Foxconn is repetitive and hard, the pressure from management unrelenting. Some workers have reported being forced to stand for twenty-four hours at a time. Others say they are beaten by their supervisors. Starting around 2010, employees at Foxconn plants in China began to kill themselves in alarming numbers.

Workers hanged themselves, took poison, jumped from windows. There was very little news coverage of any of it until 2012. That year about 150 Foxconn workers at a plant in Wuhan climbed to the roof of their factory and threatened to commit mass suicide if conditions didn't improve. The company responded by installing circus nets beneath the railings.

All pretty grim. Yet when was the last time you heard a politician decry Apple's treatment of workers, let alone introduce legislation intended to address it? When was the last time a group of socially conscious hipsters from Brooklyn protested outside the home of Apple CEO Tim Cook?

Never, of course. That's because Apple, like virtually every other big employer in American life, has purchased indulgences from the church of cultural liberalism. Apple has a gay CEO with fashionable social views. The company issues statements about green energy and has generous domestic partner benefits. Apple publicly protested the Trump administration's immigration policies. The company is progressive in ways that matter in Brooklyn. That's enough to stop any conversation about working conditions in Foxconn factories.

Indeed, the whole point is not to talk about Foxconn factories. As Notre Dame professor Patrick Deneen points out, the ruling class's "insistent defense of equality is a way of freeing themselves from any real duties to the lower classes that are increasingly out of geographical sight and mind. Because they repudiate inequality, they need not consciously consider themselves to be a ruling class."

A resolute lack of self-awareness makes this arrangement possible. Earlier ruling classes understood they were in charge. They admitted it and faced the consequences, including a responsibility to those beneath them. Noblesse oblige means "obligations of the nobility." Every functioning aristocracy has taken that obligation seriously.

The modern rich, by contrast, don't acknowledge that they're at the top of the economic heap, or even that a heap exists. They pretend they're like everyone else, just more impressive. They deny, Deneen writes, "that they really are a self-perpetuating elite that has not only inherited certain advantages but also seeks to pass them on. To mask this fact, they describe themselves as the vanguard of equality, in effect denying the very fact of their elevated status and the deleterious consequences of their perpetuation of a class divide that has left their less fortunate countrymen in a dire and perilous condition."

Meanwhile, the nameless workers whose heavily discounted labor has helped push Apple's market cap ever closer to a trillion dollars live in stinking dormitories in towns you can't pronounce and are killing themselves in desperation. And no one cares.

Forty years ago, the suffering of Chinese workers would have offended the elites' sense of decency and fairness. Rich housewives on the Upper East Side would have made a cause out of it. Celebrities would have denounced Foxconn in talk show appearances. Someone would have mentioned oppressed Chinese workers in an Oscar speech.

Today the ruling class is silent, indeed unconcerned. Liberals view Apple as the apex of tech chic. The company's business practices aren't merely tolerated, they're celebrated. College graduates compete to work in its sad, spare retail stores, wearing dopey matching T-shirts and selling laptops. This may all seem normal now, but it is a relatively new development.

In 1974, journalist Studs Terkel published a book called *Working*, an oral history of what people do for a living. Terkel was a 1930s-era socialist from Chicago, but for the most part he kept his opinions out of the book. He let his subjects speak. One man he interviewed described what it was like to be a machinist, another talked about spending his life as a doorman in an apartment building. It was a window into a world elites knew little about. But they were interested.

Working became a huge bestseller, and then a Broadway musical. James Taylor wrote part of the score. The play was nominated for five Tony Awards. Liberals loved the book because it highlighted the dignity of working people.

If *Working* came out today, how many copies would it sell in Brookline or Marin County? Not enough to justify publishing it. Unless the machinist was transitioning to a new gender or fighting immigration authorities over an expired visa, modern elites wouldn't care.

Huge corporations have displaced the blue-collar proletariat in the hearts of elites. Corporations embrace a progressive agenda that from an accounting perspective costs them nothing. In exchange, they get to maintain the economic status quo that has made them billions. The company's affluent customers get to imagine they're fighting the power by purchasing the products, even as they make a tiny group of people richer and more powerful. There's never been a more brilliant marketing strategy.

Days after a mass shooting in the summer of 2016, San Francisco–based Uber sent a message to users announcing that "our hearts go out to the victims of this week's terrible gun violence" and calling for a moment of silence to reflect upon it. For emphasis, peace signs appeared on the Uber app. "As we move around our cities this weekend, let's take a moment to think about what we can do to help," the company suggested.

One obvious thing Uber might have done to help: treat its own employees more humanely. At the very moment Uber was using its app to showcase its own decency, the corporation supervised more than one million drivers. In a traditional company, every one of these workers would be classified as an employee, which would make Uber the second-largest private-sector employer in the world. But employees are expensive. They require vacation days and health-care benefits. They have rights. In the United States, employees receive unemployment insurance, and they're entitled to compensation for on-the-job injuries.

With a value greater than the gross domestic product of some African countries, Uber could have paid for all of that. Its owners didn't want to. So instead, Uber maintained the conceit that its drivers weren't employees, but "contractors," independent small business owners who just happened to be using Uber as a way to find customers.

It was a semantic trick of incalculable value to the company, but it didn't change the fact that Uber was running an enormously valuable business on the backs of exploited workers. A 2018 study at MIT found that fully three-quarters of Uber drivers earned less than the minimum hourly wage in the states where they were driving. Almost a third of them lost money in the deal. In effect, they were paying Uber to drive.

It was a pretty good deal for Uber. The company's thirty-nine-year-old founder had a personal net worth of $5 billion.

The usual watchdogs didn't seem to notice any of this. Instead of being denounced as exploitative, Uber was lauded as a pioneer, a corporate John the Baptist heralding the arrival of a savior called the "gig economy." Low pay, no benefits, unsteady hours? Whatever. An obedient business press focused instead on the "flexibility" Uber's contractors supposedly enjoyed. Happy workers, cheerfully making America better.

An earlier generation of liberals would have recognized how awful all this is. Feudal lords took more responsibility for their serfs than Uber does for its drivers. Yet Uber executives weren't ashamed. They didn't need to be. They sold exploitation as opportunity, and virtually nobody called them on it.

Indeed when high-profile controversies did hit Uber, they had nothing to do with the company's labor practices. Outrage erupted instead over the superficial issues that now routinely inflame the modern ruling class. In January 2017, protesters chained themselves to the front doors of Uber's San Francisco headquarters. Why? Because founder and CEO Travis Kalanick had agreed to participate in a business advisory board established by President-elect Donald Trump.

In June 2017, Kalanick resigned. Once again, his perceived sins had nothing to do with how he treated his drivers, many of whom lived in poverty. Instead, Kalanick was brought down by allegations of widespread sexism at the company, a "toxic brand of corporate machismo," as the *Washington Post* put it. After Kalanick left, the *Post* ridiculed Uber for failing to replace him with a new female CEO.

The marriage of market capitalism to progressive social values may be the most destructive combination in American economic history. Someone needs to protect workers from the terrifying power of market forces, which tend to accelerate change to intolerable levels and crush the weak. For generations, labor unions filled that role. That's over. Left and right now agree that a corporation's only real responsibility is to its shareholders. Companies can openly mistreat their employees (or "contractors"), but for the price of installing transgender bathrooms they buy a pass. Shareholders win, workers lose. Bowing to the diversity agenda is a lot cheaper than raising wages.

Marissa Mayer figured this out early. A longtime Google executive, Mayer spent five years running the tech giant Yahoo. During that time she became one of the most famous business leaders in America, and definitely one of the richest. How did Yahoo do?

Under Mayer's leadership, the company's business model collapsed completely; Yahoo shed half its employees. Mayer responded by making several disastrous acquisitions. She bought the blogging platform Tumblr for more than a billion dollars, a ludicrous overvaluation.

Meanwhile, Yahoo neglected its most basic duties to customers, allowing massive privacy breaches that exposed users' personal data to hackers.

In the face of all this, Mayer mounted a public relations campaign that emphasized her role as a female pioneer in the tech business. She sat for an endless series of treacly media profiles, including a spread in the fashion magazine *Vogue*.

In the end, her tenure was a measurable disaster. Yahoo's core search business was sold to Verizon for less than $5 billion, a $95 billion discount from what it was once worth.

Yet somehow, in return for presiding over Yahoo's destruction, Mayer became richer than ever. She collected a total of $239 million in compensation from the company, $900,000 for every week she spent destroying it.

In an earlier age, this would be known as looting. The popular press would have attacked Marissa Mayer as a living symbol of incompetence and greed. Angry workers might have picketed her house. That's not what happened. Liberals celebrated Mayer as a next-generation feminist hero. She currently serves on the board of Wal-Mart.

Identity politics protected Mayer. As a progressive member of a protected group, her threshold for failure was adjusted radically upward. But that's not the only reason Mayer dodged the criticism she deserved. Liberals don't scrutinize power like they used to, probably because they now wield it.

———

Mark Zuckerberg of Facebook is richer than Andrew Carnegie ever was, but he never worked in a cotton mill. Zuckerberg grew up in an affluent New York suburb, the son of a dentist and a psychiatrist, and attended both Exeter and Harvard. From birth to the present day, Zuckerberg has never lived outside the elite culture that produced him. Fortunately for him, neither have many of his coworkers, or for that matter many of the reporters who cover him, or the lawmakers charged with regulating him. They're all from the same world.

Starting in college, Zuckerberg has been repeatedly accused of unethical business practices. Evidence has mounted that Facebook is an addictive product that harms users, and that Zuckerberg knew that from the beginning but kept selling it to unknowing consumers. Those facts would be enough to tarnish most reputations, if not spark congressional hearings. Yet Zuckerberg remains a celebrated national icon. The only people who could punish Zuckerberg are his peers, and they don't seem to notice or care.

Zuckerberg started his first Web venture in 2003 while a student at Harvard. The site was called Facemash. It compiled photos of Harvard students and allowed visitors to evaluate their attractiveness. Zuckerberg published the photos without students' permission. School administrators scolded him but let him stay at Harvard and build more websites.

Inspired by Harvard's printed student directory "face books," Zuckerberg and friends decided to create their own version online. Initially only available on campus, Facebook proved immensely popular and expanded to other elite colleges, then to all colleges, then to high school students, and finally to everyone thirteen or older.

As Facebook grew, several of Zuckerberg's early collaborators accused him of stealing credit and shares in the company. Lawsuits followed and Zuckerberg paid. But Facebook kept growing. The company now has close to two billion users world-wide. Zuckerberg is worth more than $70 billion.

From the beginning, Zuckerberg displayed contempt for his customers, even as he reveled in the power the company gave him. Just days after Facebook's launch, Zuckerberg bragged to a friend online about how he held the personal information of virtually every student on campus and offered "info about anyone at Harvard." They "trust me," Zuckerberg explained. "Dumb fucks."

Several years later, Zuckerberg assured users that they shouldn't worry about Facebook's power over them or be concerned about their lost privacy. As Zuckerberg explained, the "social norm" of privacy itself no longer existed. People no longer had any right to worry about strangers snooping on them.

Zuckerberg maintained a different standard for himself. One of the first things he did with his Facebook wealth was buy a secluded 750-acre estate in Hawaii, and then surround it with a six-foot wall. To create a privacy buffer around his house in Palo Alto, Zuckerberg bought four adjacent properties for a total of more than $30 million. Pictures show that Zuckerberg covers the webcam on his personal laptop with masking tape, for privacy reasons. Mark Zuckerberg doesn't trust tech companies.

Meanwhile, Facebook continues to gather ever-growing amounts of intimate information about its customers. Most users understand that Facebook can see everything in a given profile: photos, likes, friends. But Facebook's surveillance goes much deeper. Most people have no idea.

Use Facebook's mobile app on your phone? Facebook sees and records everywhere you go. Facebook knows the stores you visited, the events you attended, and whether you walked, drove, or rode your bike. Because Facebook is integrated onto so many other sites, the company also knows much of your Web browsing history as well, even when you're not browsing on Facebook.

By synthesizing this information, Facebook's algorithms can make astonishingly accurate assumptions about your life. After tracking where you live and what you buy online, Facebook can deduce your assets, even if you've never posted a single word on Facebook about money. Facebook's facial recognition software is now so advanced, it can detect users in uploaded photos, even if the users haven't been tagged.

This level of knowledge is what makes Facebook so valuable. Facebook knows more about its users than many spouses know about each other. Facebook sells this information to companies, which use it to make the most finely tuned advertising pitches in history. In effect, Facebook's customers are its product, the commodity it offers for sale. The company's success is based on how much time it can get users to spend staring at a screen, providing eyeballs for ads and data for the company's algorithms.

The company has been remarkably successful at winning and keeping users. In the United States and Canada, 184 million people use Facebook or its affiliated apps every day, for an average of about fifty minutes each. For many people, Facebook functions like an addiction.

There's a reason for that. In the fall of 2017, Facebook's first president, Sean Parker, gave an interview to *Axios* in which he admitted that Facebook can override the free will of its users. The product is literally addictive. It was engineered to be that way.

When engineers designed Facebook, Parker explained, they asked themselves, "'How do we consume as much of your time and conscious attention as possible?'" In order to achieve that, "we need to sort of give you a little dopamine hit every once in a while, because someone liked or commented on a photo or a post or whatever. And that's going to get you to contribute more content, and that's going to get you . . . more likes and comments."

Parker wasn't exaggerating. A study published in 2016 found that using Facebook stimulated the brain in a way similar to cocaine. Ramsay Brown, cofounder of a firm called Dopamine Labs, which uses neuroscience to makes apps more compelling, explained to a Bay Area television station that Facebook and its subsidiary Instagram use precise algorithms to time notifications and alerts to give users a maximally addictive dopamine hit.

"Sometimes there's nothing waiting for you, sometimes there's a friend request or someone wrote on your wall," Brown said. "Sometimes there's just kind of like filler crap. It's not pertinent to your life, but Facebook's algorithms have figured out that showing it to you then is going to be slightly more surprising than not showing it to you at all or showing it to you later."

In his *Axios* interview, Parker noted that Facebook wasn't just as addictive as a drug, but was having similarly wide-reaching effects.

"[Facebook] literally changes your relationship with society, with each other," he said. "God only knows what it's doing to our children's brains."

It was a stunning admission, but it received surprisingly little attention at the time. Tobacco companies spent decades making their products more addictive, but hid that fact because they feared punishment and increased government oversight. Parker had no such fears.

Indeed, Parker boasted about how rich he'd become selling an addictive product. "Because I'm a billionaire," he said, "I'm going to have access to better health care so . . . I'm going to be like 160 and I'm going to be part of this, like, class of immortal overlords."

Parker wasn't the only Facebook executive to admit the company had a destructive effect on its customers. In December 2017, former Facebook vice president Chamath Palihapitiya conceded the company had gravely injured humanity itself: "I think we have created tools that are ripping apart the social fabric of how society works," he said.

Science agrees. A 2017 study in the *American Journal of Epidemiology* found that the use of Facebook correlated with declining psychological and even physical health. The more time people spent liking posts or updating their Facebook status, the less happy they felt.

Plenty of other research discovered the same thing. One study from 2014 found heavy Facebook use was associated with eating disorders. A 2015 University of Missouri study found that Facebook made people depressed and envious from viewing the carefully curated lives of their friends. In 2016, a study found that quitting Facebook improved psychological health.

Facebook's photo-sharing site Instagram may be even worse for human well-being. A 2017 survey by the British Royal Society for Public Health found that Instagram was the most harmful of all the major social networks. Use of the app caused loneliness, anxiety over body image, and other maladies.

Facebook knows all this. It uses the knowledge to boost revenue. A leaked internal document, published by the *Australian* in 2017, noted that Facebook's internal algorithms could deduce the emotional states of users based on their behavior on the website. The company uses the information to direct ad campaigns.

Some of the emotional states the company claimed it could detect included "worthless," "defeated," "stupid," "useless," "insecure," and "failure."

Facebook is omnipresent. It is addictive, intentionally so. Its product hurts people, including children. What have America's elites done about it? Nothing. Congress has never held a hearing on social media addiction or how it's harming society. No lawmakers are even considering legislation to address any of this. Reporters couldn't be less interested.

When the media do cover Mark Zuckerberg, it's usually in an adulatory way. The *Wall Street Journal* once published a piece suggesting the country needs more of him: "How to Raise the Next Mark Zuckerberg."

Harvard president Drew Faust went even further. "Mark Zuckerberg's leadership has profoundly altered the nature of social engagement worldwide," Faust slobbered as she introduced Zuckerberg as Harvard's 2017 commencement speaker. "And few individuals can rival Mark Zuckerberg in his drive to change our world through the innovative use of technology, as well as his commitment to advance science, enhance education, and expand opportunity through the pursuit of philanthropy."

Zuckerberg seems to agree with this characterization. On his own Facebook page, Zuckerberg describes his personal mission this way: "I'm trying to make the world a more open place."

There is no mention of ripping apart the social fabric.

Tobacco companies once tried marketing like this: "More Doctors Smoke Camels Than Any Other Cigarette!" The difference is, the media called them on it.

A glowing cover story in *Time* magazine from 2014 opens with a photo of Zuckerberg surrounded by a crowd of poor children in India. "Our mission is to connect every person in the world," Zuckerberg is quoted as saying.

The article does briefly note the obvious financial interest Facebook has in hooking every living person on social media. But the piece quickly moves on to suggest that "creating wealth and saving lives" are likely Zuckerberg's real motives.

When elites do focus their attention on Facebook, it's invariably to demand the company exert even more control over its users. Following the 2016 election, there were widespread calls for Facebook to further restrict the news Americans are allowed to see on the site. According to the *Washington Post*, Barack Obama took Zuckerberg aside during a meeting of world leaders in Peru and begged him to impose greater censorship.

Democratic senator Dianne Feinstein of California made the same demand. "You created these platforms and now they are being misused," she said. "And you have to be the ones who do something about it—or we will."

If only Obama and Feinstein were as concerned about Facebook's relentless invasions of the public's privacy. Or about the millions of addicted users steadily degrading from its use. Or about the rending of the social fabric.

Perhaps in order to inoculate himself against elite criticism, Zuckerberg has immersed himself in fashionable political causes. In 2013, he launched a nonprofit called FWD.us to advocate for mass immigration. The group lobbied against immigration enforcement and pushed for amnesty for the more than 11 million illegal immigrants in the United States, complete with citizenship and voting rights.

Some of this lobbying took place in the open, in the form of op-eds and meetings on Capitol Hill. Some was more devious. In

2013, FWD.us created a satellite organization called Americans for a Conservative Direction. Its purpose was to cast support for more immigration as a conservative position. One of the group's ads was so stealthy, it didn't even mention immigration. Instead it promoted the Keystone XL pipeline, trashed Obamacare, and derided Washington's "Chicago-style politics." These ads ran on behalf of Senator Lindsey Graham of South Carolina. The point was to paint Graham as a reliable conservative, in order to give him sufficient cover with voters to support amnesty.

At the same time, FWD.us created another satellite group, this one called the Council for American Job Growth. That group attacked Republicans and framed immigration reform as a progressive cause.

When caught playing both sides against voters, FWD.us was blunt about its strategy: "Maintaining two separate entities . . . to support elected officials across the political spectrum," the group explained, "means that we can more effectively communicate with targeted audiences of their constituents." In other words, whatever it takes.

By the 2016 election, Facebook itself was producing propaganda from its headquarters in Menlo Park. Former employees told *Gizmodo* they "routinely" suppressed right-leaning stories on the company's breaking news platform. "News curators" kept stories they regarded as conservative from appearing among those trending on Facebook, even if actual share numbers indicated they were popular enough to be included.

In one case, Facebook suppressed critical stories about Lois Lerner, the IRS official who blocked conservative groups seeking nonprofit status. Facebook also spiked positive stories about Senator Ted Cruz, Wisconsin governor Scott Walker, and

Chris Kyle, the murdered Navy SEAL who was the subject of the film *American Sniper.* One conservative group found itself banned from Facebook for saying that Donald Trump did not hate Muslims.

At the same time, Facebook employees artificially promoted stories they agreed with. In one case, the company boosted coverage of the Black Lives Matter movement, even though it wasn't trending among actual Facebook users. The cause was popular enough inside the building. Zuckerberg himself endorsed Black Lives Matter in an internal message to staff. In the same memo, he condemned an employee unwise enough to write "All Lives Matter" on a company bulletin board.

For someone committed to increasing global openness, Zuckerberg has been consistently willing to abet censorship in authoritarian regimes abroad. In just six months in 2015, Facebook blocked 55,000 pieces of politically sensitive content in twenty different countries at the request of foreign governments.

In February 2018, Instagram caved to Russia's demands and censored a video made by Alexei Navalny, the most prominent anti-Putin opposition leader.

Above all, Zuckerberg has proved eager to accommodate the demands of the Chinese government. Facebook has been blocked in China since 2009, after the site was used by pro-independence activists in the region of Xinjiang, and has been working to get back in ever since. In 2016, Facebook reportedly developed a tool that would allow it to suppress posts from appearing in news feeds within certain geographic areas, presumably at the direction of Chinese government censors.

So far it hasn't been enough. Facebook still hasn't broken into China. When it does, expect Zuckerberg's many fans in the media and Congress to applaud uncritically. Bill and Hillary Clinton will doubtless send a congratulatory text.

All of which is a measure of how much American society has changed over a relatively short period.

———

There was a time when Bill and Hillary Clinton would have been deeply suspicious of Facebook and its appeasement of authoritarian regimes. The Clintons entered American politics during a period when educated young people tended to consider themselves civil libertarians and enemies of the establishment. Bill and Hillary were Nixon haters and supporters of the radical George McGovern campaign. Bill helped organize protests against Lyndon Johnson's war in Vietnam. Hillary's first major speech, to the graduating class at Wellesley College in 1969, was a broadside aimed at her school's own commencement speaker, establishment Republican senator Edward Brooke. Hillary criticized Brooke for advocating for gradual social change rather than revolutionary protest.

The Clintons no longer have these views, to put it mildly, and not just because they're older. After decades in power, Bill and Hillary have become archdefenders of the status quo, political and economic.

Hillary's 2016 presidential run resembled nothing so much as a counterinsurgency campaign, designed to beat back challenges to existing authority, specifically herself. She collaborated with party bosses to undercut her primary opponent, Bernie Sanders, who posed a threat precisely because he was more popular with the party's younger, idealistic voters. It was a cynical effort by a cynical establishment politician to retain power at any cost.

———

In one of the great ironies of American politics, it was Hillary's cynicism that undid her campaign. Warned by advisors that she needed to address middle-class economic frustration, Hillary refused. She found populist economics distasteful, and more than that, unnecessary. Voters, she assumed, would believe what they're told. So the Clinton campaign soldiered on with its original message: "Things in America are fine. It's Hillary's turn to be president. You'd have to be a bigot to oppose her." No aging potentate was ever more out of touch.

Not surprisingly, Hillary's only child is even more removed from the people she claims to advocate for. Unlike her mother, Chelsea Clinton never made the journey from rebellious young person to establishment elder. She began and stayed in the establishment. She is the living embodiment of the modern American ruling class.

Born in 1980 while her father was governor of Arkansas, Chelsea Clinton's life parallels the rise of our meritocratic elite. By twelve, she was living in the White House and enrolled at Sidwell Friends School, where the children of presidents, cabinet secretaries, and Washington journalists have gone for decades.

From Sidwell, Chelsea chose Stanford from a long list of schools eager to have her, including Harvard, Yale, Princeton, and Brown. In news stories at the time, Harvard scrambled to reassure other applicants that Chelsea "didn't have to play the daddy card" and was admitted entirely based on her own grades and test scores. Coincidentally, all four of then–vice president Al Gore's children were also admitted to Harvard, presumably also on the strength of their grades and test scores.

After finishing at Stanford, Chelsea won admission to Oxford, where she received a master's degree in international relations. The head of University College at Oxford noted that "the college is also pleased to extend its link with the Clinton family."

Soon after graduation, Chelsea won one of the most prestigious jobs in the world, at the management consulting firm McKinsey & Company. She was the youngest member of her consultant class. Despite having no experience in finance, business, or, for that matter, employment, Chelsea received the same rank as classmates who had completed MBAs. At twenty-three, she was making $120,000 a year.

She didn't stay long. Three years later, at just twenty-six, Chelsea moved to a job as a chemical industry analyst with Avenue Capital Group, a $12 billion hedge fund. Her salary at the firm wasn't public, but it would have been generous. The fund was run by longtime Clinton donor Marc Lasry.

Looking back in a 2014 interview with *Fast Company*, Chelsea downplayed the financial benefits of all this. She described her early jobs as a process of self-discovery, a kind of metaphysical experiment that allowed her to shed materialism and ascend above the sad wage-chasers around her.

"I was curious if I could care about [money] on some fundamental level, and I couldn't," she said. "That wasn't the metric of success that I wanted in my life."

To signify her commitment to a simpler existence, Chelsea and her husband bought a five-thousand-square-foot, $10 million apartment in New York City's Flatiron District. The unit was reported to be the widest apartment in New York. It stretched an entire city block.

Despite her emphatic rejection of materialism, Chelsea somehow got rich during President Obama's two terms. In 2011, she was hired as a special correspondent by NBC. To some this seemed surprising, since Chelsea had never worked in television, or as a journalist anywhere. Indeed, she had no relevant experience at all.

NBC didn't mind. The company paid Chelsea $600,000 a year, far more than other entry-level correspondents. At the time, Chelsea's mother was known to be planning a presidential run, and was considered likely to win. Chelsea's spokesperson described the NBC job as an opportunity to "serve in the public good."

Chelsea worked at NBC for just under three years. It's debatable how much public good she achieved. She did very few stories. In one segment, Chelsea flew to Kenya to visit an elephant orphanage. In another, she interviewed participants in the Foster Grandparent program. In one memorable exchange, Chelsea interviewed the animated gecko character from Geico insurance commercials. She asked the character whether he was recognized on the street.

By the time she quit to advise her mother's presidential campaign, *Business Insider* calculated that Chelsea had appeared on network television for a total of just fifty-eight minutes, less than four seconds a day. NBC paid her $26,724 for every minute she spent on the air.

But television reporting wasn't Chelsea's only source of income. In 2011, while still a student at Oxford, she joined the board of IAC/InterActiveCorp, the media conglomerate. The position paid her $50,000 a year, roughly the annual income of the average American household, plus $250,000 per year in company stock.

In a statement, IAC boasted that Chelsea's "skills and background complement the existing areas of expertise of other board members." There was no mention of what those specific skills might be. There seemed to be consensus that Chelsea was among the most talented and deserving people in the world. It's also true that the chairman of IAC's board was Barry Diller, a longtime Clinton family donor and friend.

Whatever Chelsea did on the IAC board must have been impressive, because in the spring of 2017 Diller handed her another board seat, this one at the travel company Expedia, where he is also chairman. The seat was created for her. It paid $45,000 a year, plus an annual $250,000 in stock. Not bad for someone who rejects the principle of money. Apparently good things come to those who don't seek them. Deepak's law of detachment in action.

And the money kept flowing. Chelsea began a highly lucrative sideline giving speeches. In 2015, the University of Missouri at Kansas City balked at paying Hillary's Clinton's $275,000 speaking fee. Instead the school paid Chelsea $65,000 for a brief appearance on campus. Other speeches followed.

By this point, Chelsea was busier than ever. She got a producing credit on a film about interfaith friendship. Most significantly she became vice chair of the Clinton Foundation, her family's vast nonprofit. Officially a charity, the foundation had commercial uses as well. In emails leaked during the 2016 election, former Clinton aide Doug Band complained that Chelsea and her husband, Marc Mezvinsky, used the Clinton Foundation to solicit investments for Eaglevale Partners, Mezvinsky's hedge fund. Unlike his wife, Mezvinsky never struggled to make himself care about money.

Mezvinsky did, however, struggle to earn money. Eaglevale Partners attracted several hundred million dollars in investments, including sizable sums from various Clinton donors. Mezvinsky used some of that cash to make huge bets on the future of the Greek economy. That turned out to be unwise.

By early 2016, Mezvinsky's "Hellenic Opportunity Fund" had lost 90 percent of its value. Just a month after Hillary Clinton's 2016 defeat, the entire hedge fund went under. Investors wanted their money back. In the wake of his mother-in-law's loss, Mezvinsky's financial acumen was considered diminished.

Throughout Chelsea's years in the public eye, there have been rare critics who've sniped that she is the beneficiary of cronyism and nepotism. Some accused her of playing through life on the lowest difficulty setting without even realizing it.

The media were not among these critics. They celebrated Chelsea as the stunningly accomplished woman they considered her to be. A 2013 profile in *Parade* magazine is typical:

> Clinton's concentration does not waver. She demonstrates a masterly command of the issues and swiftly zeroes in on crucial questions. Statistics roll comfortably off her tongue; praise comes as quickly as critical suggestions. Wonky words like metrics and cohort fit naturally into her carefully constructed sentences.

If you've graduated from high school, you might not consider words like "metric" and "cohort" advanced vocabulary. Editors at the *New York Times* disagree. The paper celebrated Chelsea for using the terms "anathema" and "behemoth." The site Refinery29 congratulated her for "refracted."

In 2014, *Fast Company* praised Chelsea as not only a fluent English speaker, but also a visionary innovator: "Chelsea is as

forward-thinking and open-minded as any Silicon Valley entre-
preneur of her generation."

Given all this, it wasn't surprising when *Glamour* magazine
honored Chelsea with one of its 2014 Women of the Year awards.
The prize was awarded for Chelsea's important work at the Clinton Foundation, though the magazine wasn't specific about what
that might be. There was no mention of fund-raising for her husband's hedge fund.

In the months after the 2016 election, Chelsea didn't hide or
retreat from public life. Forward-thinking entrepreneurs don't do
that. Instead she wrote a socially aware children's book, *She Per-
sisted*, which she promoted on a twelve-city tour. The publisher
described the book as aimed at "tiny feminists, mini activists and
little kids who are ready to take on the world." It's unclear how
many children read it.

By the age of thirty-six, Chelsea had been a scholar at Oxford, a top management consultant, a hedge fund wiz, a corporate director, a network television correspondent, a nonprofit
executive, a published author, a documentary filmmaker, and
a senior advisor to a presidential campaign. Short of winning
the Victoria Cross for gallantry, there wasn't much left for her to
achieve. So she became a public intellectual. Twitter was Chelsea's canvas.

The *New York Times* heralded her arrival with a story of
more than one thousand words: "Now on Twitter: Chelsea Clinton, Unbound." The paper described her as "sarcastic and feisty,"
its highest possible praise.

CNN enthusiastically concurred. "Freed from the constraints of her mother's political ambitions," the story said, Chelsea "has taken to the medium, posting frequently and weighing

in on current events with a distinctive, sometimes sassy, voice America hasn't heard before."

At *BuzzFeed*, celebrity editor Lauren Yapalater swooned with excitement. "Recently Chelsea has been addressing everything happening in our country right now with tweets that are both subtly shady and also just blunt," she wrote. Chelsea's tweets are "soul cleansing."

Ordinary Twitter readers would be forgiven for having a different reaction. Most of Chelsea's tweets were indistinguishable from the familiar brand of easily offended Acela-class elitism. Some were aggressively banal.

One read: "Words without action are . . . meaningless. Words with inaction are . . . just words. Words with opposite action is . . . hypocrisy."

In another, she reported this: "Yesterday, I saw a man in jeans and a t-shirt riding a skateboard. It was 28 degrees. Thankfully, he was also wearing a helmet."

Sassy. Soul cleansing.

But Chelsea could also be stern when necessary, especially when fellow Twitter users needed to be reminded of the Rules. In March 2017, a jewelry company ran a billboard ad joking, "Sometimes it's okay to throw rocks at girls." Meaning diamonds.

Chelsea's response: "Talking about hitting girls is never funny. Ever."

In the early months of the Trump administration, White House aide Steve Bannon was asked about the low number of televised briefings. Bannon joked that press secretary Sean Spicer had "got fatter." Chelsea swung into action.

"The White House using fat shaming to justify increased opacity. 2017," Clinton tweeted.

When another Twitter user pointed out that Bannon was joking, Chelsea summoned her signature sassiness. "Oh ok," she wrote. "So using fat shaming to avoid answering questions about increasing opacity. Got it. 2017."

The *New York Times* treated exchanges like this like the discovery of an unpublished Proust novel. The paper ran a feature on Chelsea's reading habits and book recommendations. *Elle* published a celebratory piece, "Chelsea Clinton on the Obama Girls, Overcoming Discouragement, and How We Must Empower Young Girls."

Variety put Chelsea on its cover and interviewed her about her expertise in social media. Questions included "Where does your empowerment come from?"

Also: "What were your favorite foods growing up?"

Chelsea's response revealed a lot about what her childhood must have been like: "I liked healthy food, because those were really the only foods they let me eat."

By late 2017, Chelsea was back in the pages of *Teen Vogue*. There she published an open letter to her children, which may or may not have begun as a late-night Facebook screed and in any case didn't sound like the kind of thing you'd write to your kids, or that they'd voluntarily read. *Teen Vogue* proudly ran it anyway.

In her letter, Chelsea complained about Donald Trump, came out against bullying and climate change, and fretted that transgender soldiers are no longer welcome in the military. She ended by noting that "protecting children isn't someone else's job; it's all our jobs—even if the president doesn't think it's his."

It was nothing readers hadn't seen before. What's interesting is what Chelsea didn't say. She didn't challenge the existing order, or even acknowledge its existence. She didn't wonder why an ever-shrinking number of Americans control an ever-expanding share of the country's wealth. She didn't ask why the middle class is dying, or why our society is fragmenting. She definitely didn't pause to consider how someone so thoroughly ordinary as herself could become rich and famous in a country that claims to promote on the basis of achievement.

If the meritocracy is real, why is *Teen Vogue* pretending a letter so stupefyingly conventional is brilliant? That would have been a good question.

Chelsea didn't ask. She's not interested in the answer. She has no idea she should be.

In Chelsea Clinton's world, nobody tells her she's wrong.

TWO

Importing a Serf Class

In an earlier age, American leaders never dismissed the country's population as lazy and immoral. They might have said so privately, in restaurant booths or on golf courses, and surely they did. But never in public. That would have seemed snobbish and out of touch, even anti-American. Vilifying the middle class in a middle-class country was unpatriotic.

Fifty years ago, elites understood that the point of any major government policy was to help as many Americans as possible. They often fell short of that standard, but they never challenged it. Their political heroes reflected their priorities. Most of the people they revered, even the ideologues on the hard left, were effectively populists, leaders whose main concern was the dignity and prosperity of average people.

In the American West, no populist figure was more revered

than Cesar Chavez. Chavez, an itinerant farmworker with a seventh-grade education, founded and led the United Farm Workers union. In the 1960s, Chavez led the legendary Delano grape strike, which lasted for five years and inspired college students across the country to wear "Boycott Grapes" pins.

Chavez's signature rallying cry, *"¡Si, se puede!"* ("Yes we can!"), became so famous among well-educated liberals that Barack Obama used it as a campaign slogan when he ran for president. Growing up in California, I can't remember a year when we didn't celebrate the life and achievements of Cesar Chavez in class.

Chavez's name is still everywhere in the state. There are six libraries, eleven parks, half a dozen major roads, and at least twenty-five public schools in California named after him, more than George Washington. That doesn't include the many Cesar Chavez academic buildings, student centers, and at least one college. Cesar Chavez Day is a California state holiday.

Most enduring is Chavez's *"¡Si, se puede!"* Wherever left-wing demonstrators gather, you'll hear it. It's most common at pro-immigration rallies. Several times I've seen illegal aliens scream it while carrying Mexican flags. Every time, I say a silent prayer of thanks that Cesar Chavez is long dead. It would have been torture for him.

Cesar Chavez didn't support illegal aliens. Chavez didn't like immigration at all, generally, especially the low-skilled kind. Chavez understood that new arrivals from poor countries will always work for less than Americans. Immigration hurt the members of his union, undercutting their wages and weakening their leverage in negotiations with management. Cesar Chavez believed in vigilantly defended borders. When government refused to protect them, Chavez did it himself.

In the early 1960s, Chavez fought the federal Bracero Program, which gave farmers permission to import hundreds of thousands of seasonal workers from Mexico to pick crops. Growers loved the program because it lowered their labor costs. Chavez hated it for the same reason.

Congress killed the Bracero Program in 1964, after which Chavez turned his sights on illegal aliens—or as he called them, "wetbacks." In 1969, Chavez led a march down the agricultural spine of California to protest the hiring of illegal workers by growers. Marching alongside him were future presidential candidate Walter Mondale and Reverend Ralph Abernathy, longtime aide to Martin Luther King.

By 1972, the problem of illegal labor streaming over the border had worsened. In an interview with a San Francisco television station, Chavez railed against the "wetbacks" and "illegal immigrants from Mexico" who were threatening his workers. "As long as we have a poor country bordering California, it's going to be very difficult to win strikes," he said.

When the U.S. government failed to secure the border, Chavez's unionized fruit pickers acted unilaterally. In the winter of 1979, UFW members, almost all of them Hispanic, began intercepting Mexican nationals as they crossed the border and assaulted them in the desert. Their tactics were brutal: Chavez's men beat immigrants with chains, clubs, and whips made of barbed wire. Illegal aliens who dared to work as scabs had their houses bombed and cars burned. The union paid Mexican officials to keep quiet.

In an interview with the *New York Times*, Yuma County sheriff Travis Yancey recalled watching as the UFW men set up a one-hundred-mile "wet line" of military tents along the

Arizona–Mexico border. "Each tent was manned by five or six of their people who were paid $5 to $7 day, plus their grub," said Yancey. "They'd catch any 'wet' coming through and beat the hell out of them."

Chavez didn't deny any of this. Yes, there was a union "wet line" along the border, he said. "It cost us a lot of money, and we stopped a lot of illegals."

At one union meeting, which was tape-recorded, a UFW official confronted Chavez about using the terms "illegals" and "wetback." Chavez responded angrily. "No, a spade's a spade," he said. "You guys get these hang-ups. Goddamn it, how do we build a union? They're wets, you know. They're wets, and let's go after them."

Chavez was blunter than most, but his views weren't unusual in the American labor movement. Union leaders had opposed mass immigration since the 1860s. The Chinese Exclusion Act of 1882, which banned the immigration of Chinese laborers, is often cited as an example of race hatred and xenophobia, and it may have been. But fundamentally it was a form of protectionism. The Knights of Labor backed it, and when the law came up for reauthorization in 1901, so did the American Federation of Labor.

Thanks to lobbying from unions, the Chinese Exclusion Act remained the law for more than sixty years.

Many similar laws followed. In 1885, Congress passed a measure that forbade companies from hiring foreign contract workers. Two years later, the government tightened vetting of immigrants at ports of entry. In 1888, Congress mandated fines for companies that hired illegals. All these bills were backed by organized labor.

In 1917, the American Federation of Labor successfully pushed for literacy tests for foreign workers, which had the (fully intended) effect of restricting immigration from eastern and southern European countries. Samuel Gompers, the famed AFL leader who was himself an immigrant, explained that "immigration is working a great injury to the people of our country."

For most of the twentieth century, organized labor remained skeptical of immigration. In the 1950s, the AFL merged with the Congress of Industrial Organizations, creating the modern AFL-CIO. After the merger, the union adopted a position friendly to modest legal immigration, but remained sharply opposed to illegal immigration, which it rightly saw as a vehicle for both suppressing wages and undermining organized labor.

Throughout this era, organized labor was firmly aligned with the Democratic Party, and Democrats in turn took positions on immigration that at least acknowledged the concerns of American wage earners. Democrats opposed illegal immigration and worried about the consequences of legal immigration. They believed assimilation was important.

In 1975, Governor Jerry Brown of California opposed the admission of hundreds of thousands of Vietnamese boat people after the fall of Saigon. Julia Taft ran the resettlement effort for the Ford administration. In an interview with NPR decades later, Taft recalled the pushback she received from Brown, famous at the time as one of America's most liberal politicians. Brown, Taft said, "didn't want any of these refugees, because [California] had unemployment. They already had a large number of foreign-born people there. They said they had too many Hispanics, too many people on welfare. They didn't want these people."

Jerry Brown said pretty much the same thing himself to the *Los Angeles Times*: "There is something a little strange about saying, 'Let's bring in 500,000 more people' when we can't take care of the one million [Californians] out of work." For Brown, the obligation to citizens already in California came first.

Senator Joe Biden of Delaware agreed; he introduced legislation to curb the arrival of Vietnamese immigrants, accusing the Ford administration of not being honest about how many refugees would be arriving.

Senator Robert Byrd of West Virginia was even more direct. Exactly one week after the last helicopter lifted off from the roof of the U.S. embassy in Saigon, Byrd demanded extreme vetting of Vietnamese refugees, in order to cull the "barmaids, prostitutes, and criminals."

Even George McGovern, the Democratic nominee who lost forty-nine states to Richard Nixon, opposed opening the gates. "I think the Vietnamese are better off in Vietnam," he said.

This attitude was once conventional in the Democratic Party. Nobody doubted that an influx of refugees would harm American workers. One study, conducted after the Mariel boatlift of 1980, found that Americans with lower education levels in Miami saw their wages fall by 37 percent after the Cuban refugees arrived. Modern Democrats wax enthusiastic about the virtues of economic competition, but that's an idea they borrowed fairly recently from libertarians. Nobody on the left was saying that at the time.

Here's how one prominent Democrat described his position on immigration in 1995: "All Americans, not only in the states most heavily affected but in every place in this country, are rightly disturbed by the large numbers of illegal aliens entering our country. The jobs they hold might otherwise be held by U.S. citizens or immigrants. The public services they use impose burdens on our taxpayers."

The speaker? President Bill Clinton, addressing Congress in his State of the Union speech.

Pat Buchanan never put it more succinctly.

Clinton went on to boast about hiring more Border Patrol officers, cutting off welfare for illegal immigrants, and cracking down on employers who hired illegal workers. He called for speedier deportations of illegal immigrants. "It is wrong and ultimately self-defeating for a nation of immigrants to permit the kind of abuse of our immigration laws that we've seen in recent years," Clinton said. "We must do more to stop it." He got a standing ovation.

At one point in his speech, Clinton cited Barbara Jordan, the civil rights figure and former congresswoman from Texas who was then the chair of the U.S. Commission on Immigration Reform. Jordan was an enthusiastic Democrat. She gave the opening speech at Richard Nixon's impeachment hearings. Nobody confused Jordan with a right-winger. At the time, a restrictionist position on immigration wasn't considered incompatible with liberalism.

In 1994, Jordan noted that "it is both a right and a responsibility of a democratic society to manage immigration so that it serves the national interest." The next year, she launched a broadside against multiculturalism in the pages of the *New York Times*. "Those who choose to come here must embrace the common core of American civic culture," she wrote. "We must assist them in learning our common language: American English."

Jordan didn't oppose all immigration, but she demanded

"Americanization," which she described as uniting "immigrants and their descendants around a commitment to democratic ideals and constitutional principles." For immigrants who refused to participate, Jordan supported swift deportation. Today, Jordan's views would be dismissed as racist, but they were unremarkable at the time. In 1994, Bill Clinton awarded Jordan the Presidential Medal of Freedom.

As late as 2006, there were still *New York Times* columnists willing to concede that immigration came with a downside. "Immigration reduces the wages of domestic workers who compete with immigrants," economist Paul Krugman wrote that year in the paper. "We'll need to reduce the inflow of low-skill immigrants." That same year, Hillary Clinton voted in support of a fence on the Mexican border. So did Barack Obama, Chuck Schumer, and twenty-three other Senate Democrats.

But that was the last gasp of a dying elite consensus. Consider two Democratic platforms, written just four years apart. In the 2000 platform, the Democratic Party was broadly pro-immigration but still recognized the many downsides of not adequately controlling its flow.

"Democrats believe in an effective immigration system that balances a strong enforcement of our laws with fair and even-handed treatment of immigrants and their families," the platform said. It boasted that the Clinton administration had drastically improved immigration enforcement and cut down on abuses of the asylum process. Illegal immigration was condemned for taxing government services, harming local communities, and hurting American workers.

In places, the 2000 Democratic platform sounded similar to what Donald Trump would advocate just fifteen years later. "We must punish employers who engage in a pattern and practice of recruiting undocumented workers in order to intimidate and exploit them," it said. "We believe that any increases in H1-B visas must be temporary [and] must address only genuine shortages of highly skilled workers." The platform vowed to protect American farmworkers, not just foreign pickers imported to replace them.

In a single presidential cycle, everything changed.

In 2004, gone were concerns about protecting U.S. workers, stemming a torrent of illegal border crossings, or punishing employers reliant on illegal workers. Instead, the 2004 Democratic platform called for an amnesty for illegal immigrants and a path to citizenship. Vows to protect the border focused only on keeping out terrorists, drugs, and weapons, not on illegal immigrants themselves.

The 2008 platform went even further. Now, not only did the party demand an amnesty for current illegal immigrants, but it also called for an across-the-board hike in immigration visas for both family members and skilled workers.

The Democratic Party now endorsed unrestrained mass immigration.

Remarkably, after almost 150 years of fighting for tighter labor markets, organized labor went along with most of this. In 2000, the AFL-CIO called for eliminating all sanctions on employers who deliberately hired illegal immigrants. The union also called for a total amnesty on the estimated six million illegals already in the country.

By 2016, when the Democrats faced off against Donald Trump, there were virtually no immigration skeptics remaining on the left. The same politicians and intellectuals who had once acknowledged a need to enforce the border and protect workers now disavowed their old views and suggested those who still held them were racist. The Democratic Party had given up trying to represent the working class, in favor of investors and welfare recipients—and by 2016, illegal immigrants.

In the 2016 Democratic platform, the party reframed immigration from a debate about economics to the next frontier in the struggle for civil rights and social justice. Any references to the effect of immigration on American citizens were deleted. According to the Democratic Party, the goal of immigration policy was to ensure the well-being of immigrants. "The current quota system," the platform explained, "discriminates against certain immigrants, including immigrants of color."

It's hard to think of a claim more at odds with numerical reality. In 2016, only about 18 percent of immigrants to the United States were white. Thanks almost entirely to immigration, the population of the country had gone from 84 percent white in 1965, when Congress stopped favoring European immigrants, to 62 percent white in 2015, and the number was dropping every year. There are a lot of things you could call American immigration law, but the product of white racism isn't one of them.

Twenty years after Bill Clinton told Americans they had the right to be upset about illegal immigration, his wife scolded the country for enforcing border controls. The 2016 platform demanded that all 11 million illegal immigrants living in the United States be "incorporated completely into our society through legal processes that give meaning to our national motto: E Pluribus Unum."

It was a stunning shift. It was now Democratic Party orthodoxy to give illegal immigrants, all of whom entered the country in defiance of U.S. law, the right to vote. If you had a problem with that, you were betraying the fundamental promise of the country.

The change was purely a product of political calculation. Democrats understood that the overwhelming majority of immigrant voters would vote Democrat. Surveys showed they were right.

Ironically, the more fully Democrats embraced open borders, the closer they came to where the leaders of the Republican Party had long been. Paul Ryan was elected Speaker of the House in the fall of 2015, at about the same time Trump began his run for president. Once Trump won, it was Ryan's job to translate the new president's campaign promises into workable legislation. Unfortunately for Trump and the voters who supported him, Ryan had no intention of doing that. On immigration, Ryan agreed with Democrats.

Ryan spent the early 1990s in Washington working for former Buffalo congressman Jack Kemp, one of the most aggressively pro-immigration Republicans in the House. During his time in Kemp's office, Ryan watched the voters of California approve Proposition 187, which barred illegal aliens from receiving state welfare benefits. Ryan was appalled. He and Kemp led Republican opposition to the law. When *National Review* attacked Kemp for this, Ryan authored a four-thousand-word rebuttal.

In 1996, Congress debated a bipartisan proposal to significantly curb immigration. By this point, Ryan was an aide to Representative Sam Brownback of Kansas, and he worked overtime to kill the bill. Ryan authored a series of "Dear Colleague" letters that successfully frightened Republicans into neutering the legislation.

Two years later, Ryan himself was elected to the House.

Republican voters became steadily more suspicious of mass immigration during the George W. Bush years, and Ryan at times pretended to agree with them. But it was never a comfortable pose. In 2013, Ryan made an appearance alongside Democrat Luis Gutierrez, probably the most consistent advocate for open borders in Washington, and argued that without high levels of immigration, the rule of law would vanish from America.

"We need to let legal immigrants come here legally," Ryan said. "We can't have a system where we pay homage and adherence to the rule of law if we don't have an open system where people can come here in search of their American dream, where the work that won't be done by people who are already here can be filled by the people who want to come here and do those jobs."

In 2015, Ryan said it would be wrong for the United States to take any efforts to curb Muslim immigration into the United States, because "[t]hat's not who we are." He did not elaborate.

After the 2016 election, Ryan did his best to portray himself as an immigration hawk aligned with Trump. He publicly committed to funding a border wall. His staff even produced a video backed with techno music that showed Ryan flying over the border. Message: we're going to secure this thing.

He didn't mean it. During the first year of the administration, Ryan achieved his primary goal, a massive corporate tax cut. After that, he seemed to lose interest in borders. In March 2018, Ryan produced a $1.3 trillion spending bill designed to keep the federal government funded and open. More clearly than any video Ryan's staff could shoot, the bill reflected elite Republican views on immigration.

Ryan's bill actively restricted the hiring of additional Immigration and Customs Enforcement agents for immigration enforcement. It capped the number of illegal aliens ICE could detain at any one time. It ostensibly allocated $1.6 billion for border security, but the money was explicitly prohibited from being spent on any sort of border wall.

The bill did pay for border security, just not in America. Lebanon, Jordan, Egypt, and Tunisia all received American tax dollars to deal with their immigration problems. Also included was $10 million to hire female law enforcement officers in Afghanistan, $10 million for disadvantaged students in Egypt, and $12 million to boost the military capacity of Vietnam. China, whose economy is now larger than America's, received $15 million in development aid, to promote yak herding in Tibet. Also, Congress gave itself a pay raise.

The message couldn't have been clearer: Republicans in Congress don't care about the territorial integrity of the country they run. Democratic leaders share this view. Hundreds of U.S. municipalities run by Democrats have declared themselves "sanctuary cities," barring police from cooperating in any way with federal authorities in enforcing immigration statutes, even against immigrants caught breaking U.S. law. The attorney general of California announced it is now illegal for private citizens in the state to assist federal immigration authorities in any way. Violators will be prosecuted.

In Oregon, a county judge allowed an illegal immigrant caught driving under the influence to leave the courthouse via her personal chambers, so that he could evade ICE agents. An investigation later cleared the judge of wrongdoing, on the grounds that she didn't know the man was an illegal immigrant, even though she knew he was attempting to avoid immigration authorities.

The changes in elite consensus have been so swift that some longtime politicians have struggled to keep up. In 2015, Democratic presidential candidate Bernie Sanders sat for a largely friendly interview with the publication *Vox*. *Vox* editor Ezra Klein suggested that, if Sanders wanted to curb global poverty, he should endorse unlimited migration to the United States. Sanders already supported amnesty, sanctuary cities, and continued mass immigration, but this was too much even for him. Sanders responded that open borders would "make everyone in America poorer" by driving down wages and taxing social welfare systems, all in the interest of pleasing business owners.

For this, Sanders was denounced as a bigot who didn't understand basic economics. "Bernie Sanders's fear of immigrant labor is ugly—and wrongheaded," announced a headline on *Vox*.

In the spring of 2017, the *New York Times* ran a story about a town in northwest Iowa called Storm Lake. Tyson Foods operates slaughterhouses and meatpacking plants in Storm Lake, and over the years thousands of workers from Asia and Latin America have moved there to work in them. Not surprisingly, the flood of cheap labor destroyed the local labor union and depressed wages. The *Times* interviewed one Tyson employee whose hourly wage had remained at $16 an hour for thirty-seven years.

What's striking is how the *Times* interpreted all of this. Twenty years before, the story might have been framed as a victory of management over labor. The *Times* presented it as a win for progress and diversity: "While more than 88 percent of the state's population is non-Hispanic white, less than half of Storm Lake's is. Walk through the halls of the public schools and you can hear as many as 18 languages." Mass immigration, reporter Patricia Cohen concluded, had kept the "Iowa meatpacking town alive and growing." Third-world immigration saves another American town!

Media coverage has been remarkably consistent in the way it presents the abrupt demographic change wrought by immigration. A 2018 story in *National Geographic* about Hazleton, Pennsylvania, is typical of the genre. In the year 2000, the story explained, Hazleton was 95 percent white and less than 5 percent Hispanic. Just sixteen years later, 52 percent of Hazleton residents were Hispanic. Less than half spoke English at home. People who grew up there didn't recognize the city. They didn't hate immigrants. Most Americans don't. But they were bewildered.

National Geographic's verdict: "Hazleton was another former coal mining town slipping into decline until a wave of Latinos arrived."

In Storm Lake, mass immigration had a dramatic effect on violent crime rates, which are 56 percent higher than in the rest of the state. The *New York Times* story downplayed that fact, along with the sagging performance of the local schools. The villain of the piece was Storm Lake's anti-immigration congressman, Steve King, whom the paper dismissed as a racist for opposing "cultural diversity."

The same story, written using the same set of facts, could have been a PR disaster for Tyson Foods—a multinational corporation brings in cheap labor to undercut collective bargaining. The union fails. Profits soar, while wages fall. Workers don't make enough to live, so public services take up the slack. Taxpayers wind up involuntarily subsidizing corporate profits. Tyson's shareholders get richer, while everyone else suffers.

Newspapers used to write stories like that, back before American elites decided that criticizing immigration was worse than hurting workers. Now complaints about demographic change, when they're even reported, are always dismissed as products of irrational racial fear. White anxiety. Suburban racism.

This is unfair, but it's also a smokescreen. In fact mass immigration tends to affect black neighborhoods most profoundly. Until fairly recently, Compton, California, was the largest black community west of the Mississippi. Today only a third of Compton's population is black. The rest is Hispanic. Unless you happen to drive through, you're unlikely to know that. Demographic change in Compton is the subject of relatively few news stories.

One place notably unaffected by demographic change is any neighborhood policy makers happen to live in. The people making immigration policy tend not to be affected by it. Los Angeles County, for example, is now overwhelmingly Hispanic. Upper-income Malibu, meanwhile, is still 87 percent white. New York is a diverse city, but former mayor Michael Bloomberg's zip code isn't. His neighborhood is 82 percent white, and less than 5 percent Hispanic. It's still 1985 where Bloomberg lives, and will likely always be.

Barack Obama's new zip code in Washington is less than 8 percent Hispanic. The suburbs across the river in Virginia become more Spanish-speaking every year. Obama approves of that. He sees it as a sign of progress. He doesn't want to live near it. Diversity for thee, but not for me.

The more abstract our elites' commitment to diversity becomes, the more deeply it is cherished and defended. Diversity matters more than anything. When the realities of mass immigration conflict with other elite concerns—preserving the environment, for example—elites choose immigration. Consider the case of John Tanton.

Tanton is a retired physician from Michigan and a lifelong progressive. He helped to found local chapters of both the Sierra Club and Planned Parenthood, and in general supported the agenda of the Democratic Party. That began to change in 1965, when Congress rewrote immigration law. As millions and then tens of millions of immigrants entered the United States, Tanton started to worry about the effect of all those people on the environment.

Others were concerned about that, too. In 1979, Tanton started the Federation for American Immigration Reform, with the help of investor Warren Buffett and Democratic senator Eugene McCarthy. The group argued that higher population levels would lead to more consumption, more pollution, and more environmental degradation.

Tanton imagined that others like him would join the effort to slow mass immigration. In the words of a *New York Times* profile, Tanton "hoped to enlist unions concerned about wage erosion, environmentalists concerned about pollution and sprawl, and blacks concerned about competition for housing, jobs and schools." That's not what happened.

Instead, the Southern Poverty Law Center, which fraudulently poses as a civil rights group used by the left to smear its opposition, devoted an entire page on its website to suggesting Tanton was a Nazi. "Tanton has for decades been at the heart of the white nationalist scene," the SPLC charged, providing no evidence. Tanton, who lives in a nursing home and is suffering from Parkinson's disease, could do little to defend himself.

Warren Buffett was gone by this point, reinvented as an advocate for a borderless world. Major environmental groups didn't say a word to defend Tanton, either. Even executives at the Sierra

Club, which Tanton had long supported, refused to speak up on his behalf. They'd changed their views on immigration too.

For years, the Sierra Club had articulated a zero-population-growth position. "Immigration to the U.S. should be no greater than that which will permit achievement of population stabilization in the U.S." is how the club put it in 1989.

A few years later, a California investment fund billionaire named David Gelbaum began giving money to the group, ultimately at least $200 million. Gelbaum was a pro-immigration activist who had spent heavily in an effort to defeat Proposition 187 in California. When the initiative passed anyway, Gelbaum funded the court challenge that ultimately struck it down.

Under pressure from Gelbaum, the Sierra Club radically changed its position on immigration. A battle within the organization ensued. Among the board members who objected to the change was the former Democratic governor of Colorado, Richard Lamm, and Frank Morris, the former executive director of the Congressional Black Caucus Foundation. In 2004, the *New York Times* quoted a Southern Poverty Law Center official who suggested that anyone who opposed the Sierra Club's new support for open borders was in league with racists and white nationalists.

Morris, who is black, was shocked by the slur. "To have this considered a position as a front for racists and Nazis is beyond the pale," he wrote. The paper issued a correction of sorts: "Mr. Morris disputes those characterizations, saying his support for limiting immigration reflects concerns among African-Americans and others that unchecked immigration had hurt their economic opportunities."

But the damage was done. One of America's most powerful

environmental organizations now supported mass immigration. In 2013, the group came out in favor of Barack Obama's amnesty orders. What did amnesty have to do with the environment?

As a Sierra Club spokesman explained to *Politico*, illegal immigrants "are the most adversely affected by pollution." He did not explain what that meant.

The Sierra Club's position on immigration seems to become more activist every year. In 2016, the Texas chapter of the group refused to participate in an Earth Day festival because it included participants who wanted tighter border controls. The *Austin American-Statesman,* which first reported the story, dutifully noted that anti-immigration organizations were connected to "white nationalists" through their ties to John Tanton. "We consider them hate groups," explained Sierra Club state director Reggie James. "It's Earth Day; it's not This-Side-of-the-Border Day."

By redefining immigration as a moral issue, elites have shut down debate over its costs. That's helpful for them, since for the affluent, immigration has few costs and many upsides. Low-skilled immigrants don't compete in upscale job markets. Not many recent arrivals from El Salvador are becoming lawyers or green energy lobbyists. An awful lot of them are becoming housekeepers. Mass immigration makes household help affordable. That's one of the main reasons elites support it.

From the 1800s through the 1950s, maids, nannies, gardeners, and other domestic help were ubiquitous in upper-middle-class households. Economic prosperity gradually eliminated the huge pool of unskilled labor that filled these jobs, but modern immigration policy has revived America's servant class. Immigrants now fill countless jobs as nannies, gardeners, cooks, and housekeepers.

For employers, the best part of the new arrangement is that there's no guilt attached. Let's say you lived in an affluent household in Boston in 1910. You've got help at home; everyone in your neighborhood does. The problem is, your servants are Irish. They may do a fine job making breakfast and ironing the sheets, but you can never quite relax. These are people who speak your language and look like you. At some point you may wonder: why is someone who could be my cousin cleaning my toilet? It's uncomfortable.

Third-world immigration solves this problem. When your housekeeper is a peasant from Honduras, there's no reason to feel bad about it. You don't have to wonder about the details of her life outside of work. You can barely communicate with her. She may be cleaning your floors for minimum wage (or less) while your children travel abroad, but you're not exploiting her. Just the opposite. You're giving her a hand up, allowing her to participate in the American dream.

If she's here illegally, maybe you help her get a green card. Yes, you've got an awful lot of power over her, but you're doing the right thing and you can tell your friends about it at dinner. You're not like some Saudi prince or nineteenth-century plutocrat, taking advantage of a helpless peon for your own comfort. You're compassionate. You're the hero of this story.

It's the perfect arrangement. You get to feel virtuous for having a housekeeper; she walks the dog while you're at SoulCycle. You can see why affluent moms tended to hate Donald Trump and his talk about building a wall. For Americans in the top 20 percent of income distribution, mass immigration is one of the best things that ever happened—cheap help, obedient employees, more interesting restaurants, and all without guilt. There's no downside, at least none that you personally experience.

You don't take the bus or use the emergency room for health care or send your kids to overpopulated public schools that have canceled gym and music to pay for ESL because half the kids can't speak English. The *New York Times* tells you that immigrants are reviving dying towns all over America. It's easy to imagine that only bigots would oppose open borders.

Occasionally you'll read a story about stagnant wages in the Rust Belt, or about high levels of black teen unemployment. As someone who took Econ 101 in college, you might wonder if immigration plays a role in that. You know about supply and demand, so you understand that an overabundance of anything causes its value to fall. That's why the fracking boom crashed oil prices, and why printing money causes inflation. It's why sand is cheap. So, does the same hold true for labor markets?

No, your neighbors assure you. Immigration is the one exception to the most basic law of economics. It increases the size of the economic pie, allowing everyone to benefit. It's like magic. You're happy to believe that.

Over time, you find your attitudes about the working class changing. You think of yourself as a champion of the little guy, but who's really the underdog here? The unemployed machinist in Toledo? He's fat, smokes cigarettes, and gets by on disability payments for a back injury that may or may not be legitimate. He likely voted for Donald Trump. You don't even want to know his views on gay marriage.

Compare him to your gardener. There's a guy you can admire. He somehow made it from Oaxaca to your front yard, enduring risks and privations you can only imagine, and yet he never complains, at least not in a language you can speak. He shows up on time, does a fine job, and doesn't charge much. Every month he sends money back to his family in Mexico. Why is he not more impressive than the reactionary machinist in Ohio?

He is, of course. Once you recognize that, your perspectives change. America's lower classes look less like fellow citizens, in need of uplift, and more like damaged raw materials, worthy of replacement if they aren't measuring up. Your support for social improvement efforts, the ones that previous generations of elites devoted their lives to, begins to wane.

Public schools, for example. Sure they're bad. You know that. That's why you don't send your kids. But can we really improve them? You're starting to wonder. Maybe it's just simpler to import a new wave of low-skilled workers from abroad. They certainly have better attitudes.

Even at the higher end of the income scale this is true. You love the idea of retraining out-of-work Michigan autoworkers to code software, but let's be realistic. Are they actually capable of that? It might be easier just to hire coders in Bangalore and bring them here. They'd be grateful for the chance. And isn't that the point of America anyway, to give opportunity to the world? There's a poem on the Statue of Liberty that says something like that. It's basically in the Constitution.

Once you start thinking like this, it doesn't take long to run out of empathy for your fellow Americans. In 2016, a study by the Centers for Disease Control and Prevention determined that the life expectancy of native-born Americans in many parts of the country was in decline. People were dying younger, and for reasons that were largely preventable: cirrhosis, diabetes, drug overdoses. Nothing like this had ever happened in American history. As a matter of social policy, it was a disaster. If your people are dying younger, you are failing.

How did Washington respond? With a shrug. There was a short flurry of concerned op-eds in the first week or two after the CDC report appeared. After that, silence.

It's impossible to imagine a similar reaction if the same thing were happening to Syrian refugees. They came here for a better life but instead met an early death? That wouldn't stand. There would be comprehensive news coverage of the tragedy, frothy editorials, a series of emotional speeches from the floor of the House, followed by an armada of congressional task forces that, in the end, would likely blame racism.

Our ruling class would be upset. They'd consider it, correctly, a stain on the conscience of the country.

Immigrants matter to elites. America's struggling middle class, not so much. As it happens, many employers feel the same way.

It's hard to blame the Chamber of Commerce for supporting unrestrained immigration. Businesses benefit from it, at least in the short term. Capitalists push for what's best for markets. But what happens when nobody in power takes the opposing view? We don't need to speculate.

At a closed-door speech in 2013, Hillary Clinton told a group of Brazilian bankers, "My dream is a hemispheric common market, with open trade and open borders."

Suddenly the liberal position and the conservative position were indistinguishable. It was the beneficiaries of cheap labor against everyone else. Rulers versus serfs.

THREE

Foolish Wars

One thing that every late-stage ruling class has in common is a high tolerance for mediocrity. Standards decline, the edges fray, but nobody in charge seems to notice. They're happy in their sinecures and getting richer. In a culture like this, there's no penalty for being wrong. The talentless prosper, rising inexorably toward positions of greater power, and breaking things along the way. It happened to the Ottomans. Max Boot is living proof that it's happening in America.

Boot is a professional foreign policy expert, a job category that doesn't exist outside of a select number of cities. Boot has degrees from Berkeley and Yale, and is a fellow at the Council on Foreign Relations. He has written a number of books and countless newspaper columns on foreign affairs and military history. The International Institute for Strategic Studies, an influential

British think tank, describes Boot as one of the "world's leading authorities on armed conflict."

None of this, it turns out, means anything. The professional requirements for being one of the world's Leading Authorities on Armed Conflict do not include relevant experience with armed conflict. Leading authorities on the subject don't need a track record of wise assessments or accurate predictions. All that's required are the circular recommendations of fellow credential holders. If other Leading Authorities on Armed Conflict induct you into their ranks, you're in. That's good news for Max Boot.

Boot first became famous in the weeks after 9/11 for outlining a response that the Bush administration seemed to read like a script, virtually word for word. While others were debating whether Kandahar or Kabul ought to get the first round of American bombs, Boot was thinking big. In October 2001, he published a piece in the *Weekly Standard* titled "The Case for American Empire."

"The September 11 attack was a result of insufficient American involvement and ambition," Boot wrote. "The solution is to be more expansive in our goals and more assertive in their implementation." In order to prevent more terror attacks in American cities, Boot called for a series of U.S.-led revolutions around the world, beginning in Afghanistan and moving swiftly to Iraq.

"Once we have deposed Saddam, we can impose an American-led, international regency in Baghdad, to go along with the one in Kabul," Boot wrote. "To turn Iraq into a beacon of hope for the oppressed peoples of the Middle East: Now that would be a historic war aim. Is this an ambitious agenda? Without a doubt. Does America have the resources to carry it out? Also without a doubt."

In retrospect, Boot's words are painful to read, like love letters from a marriage that ended in divorce. Iraq remains a smoldering mess. The Afghan war is still in progress close to twenty years in. For perspective, Napoleon Bonaparte seized control of France, crowned himself emperor, defeated four European coalitions against him, invaded Russia, lost, was defeated and exiled, returned, and was defeated and exiled a second time, all in less time than the United States has spent trying to turn Afghanistan into a stable country.

Things haven't gone as planned. What's remarkable is that despite all the failure and waste and deflated expectations, defeats that have stirred self-doubt in the heartiest of men, Boot has remained utterly convinced of the virtue of his original predictions. Certainty is a prerequisite for Leading Authorities on Armed Conflict.

In the spring of 2003, with the war in Iraq under way, Boot began to consider new countries to invade. He quickly identified Syria and Iran as plausible targets, the latter because it was "less than two years" from building a nuclear bomb. North Korea made Boot's list as well. Then Boot became more ambitious. Saudi Arabia could use a democracy, he decided.

"If the U.S. armed forces made such short work of a hardened goon like Saddam Hussein, imagine what they could do to the soft and sybaritic Saudi royal family," Boot wrote.

The Bush administration apparently ignored this suggestion, but Boot was undeterred. Five years later, in a piece for the *Wall Street Journal*, he advocated for the military occupation of Pakistan and Somalia. The only potential problem, he predicted, was unreasonable public opposition to new wars.

"Ragtag guerrillas have proven dismayingly successful in

driving out or neutering international peacekeeping forces," he wrote. "Think of American and French troops blown up in Beirut in 1983, or the 'Black Hawk Down' incident in Somalia in 1993. Too often, when outside states do agree to send troops, they are so fearful of casualties that they impose rules of engagement that preclude meaningful action."

In other words, the tragedy of foreign wars isn't that Americans die, but that too few Americans are willing to die. To solve this problem, Boot recommended recruiting foreign mercenaries. "The military would do well today to open its ranks not only to legal immigrants but also to illegal ones," he wrote in the *Los Angeles Times*. When foreigners get killed fighting for America, he noted, there's less political backlash at home.

American forces, documented or not, never occupied Pakistan, but by 2011 Boot had another war in mind. "Qaddafi Must Go," Boot declared in the *Weekly Standard*. In Boot's telling, the Libyan dictator had become a threat to the American homeland. "The only way this crisis will end—the only way we and our allies can achieve our objectives in Libya—is to remove Qaddafi from power. Containment won't suffice."

In the end, Gaddafi was removed from power, with ugly and long-lasting consequences. Boot was on to the next invasion. By late 2012, he was once again promoting attacks on Syria and Iran, as he had nine years before. In a piece for the *New York Times*, Boot laid out "Five Reasons to Intervene in Syria Now." Not surprisingly, all of them were simple and compelling.

Overthrowing the Assad regime, Boot predicted, would "diminish Iran's influence" in the region, influence that had grown dramatically since the Bush administration took Boot's advice and overthrew Saddam Hussein, Iran's most powerful counterbalance. To doubters concerned about a complex new war, Boot promised the Syria intervention could be conducted "with little risk."

Days later, Boot wrote a separate piece for *Commentary* magazine calling for American bombing of Iran. It was a busy week, even by the standards of a Leading Authority on Armed Conflict. In the *Commentary* piece, Boot conceded that "it remains a matter of speculation what Iran would do in the wake of such strikes." He didn't seem worried.

Listed in one place, Boot's many calls for U.S.-led war around the world come off as a parody of mindless warlike noises, something you might write if you got mad at a country while drunk. ("I'll invade you!!!") Republicans in Washington didn't find any of it amusing. They were impressed. Boot became a top foreign policy advisor to John McCain's presidential campaign in 2008, to Mitt Romney in 2012, and to Marco Rubio in 2016. He continued to churn out well-received articles for *Foreign Policy*, the *Wall Street Journal*, *USA Today*, and the *Washington Post*.

Everything changed when Trump won the Republican nomination. Trump had never heard of the International Institute for Strategic Studies. He had no idea Max Boot was a Leading Authority on Armed Conflict. Trump was running against more armed conflicts. He had no interest in invading Pakistan. Boot hated him.

As Trump found himself accused of improper ties to Vladimir Putin, Boot agitated for more aggressive confrontation with Russia. Boot demanded larger weapons shipments to Ukraine. He called for effectively expelling Russia from the global financial system, a move that might be construed as an act of war against a nuclear-armed power. The stakes were high, but with signature aplomb Boot assured readers it was "hard to imagine" the Russian government would react badly to the provocation. Those who disagreed Boot dismissed as "cheerleaders" for Putin and the mullahs in Iran.

As Boot's posture on Russia became more reckless and bellicose, his stock in the Washington foreign policy establishment rose. In 2018, he was hired by the *Washington Post* as a columnist. The paper's announcement cited Boot's "expertise on armed conflict."

———

A generation ago, it would have been hard to imagine a newspaper like the *Washington Post* celebrating Max Boot. Liberals were stridently antiwar. Opposing armed conflict was central to their identity. They hated violence; they visualized world peace. Liberals imagined a day when schools were fully funded but the Pentagon would be forced to hold bake sales, because war was not the answer and an eye for an eye made the whole world blind.

Those were actual slogans, and you heard them a lot. Liberals composed songs about peace, held festivals and symposia to celebrate it. Bumper stickers with antiwar slogans festooned the back of virtually every Volkswagen on every street in every college town in America. Mahatma Gandhi and Martin Luther King were revered on the left, not just because they were for civil rights and against colonialism, but because they were both outspoken pacifists, something that's rarely noted today. To be liberal meant to oppose violence, especially violence committed by the U.S. military.

More than anything else, liberals were turned against war by the country's experience in Vietnam. Unlike any American war before or since, Vietnam demonstrated the horror, futility, and ruin wrought by a conflict begun without domestic consensus or clear objectives. Americans were horrified by tens of thousands of military deaths and by the sight of young men drafted to go fight in a poor, distant country that posed no obvious threat to the United States. Though military leaders promised the final victory was imminent, the war dragged on for more than a decade.

Worst of all, it wasn't always clear that America held the moral high ground. South Vietnam's corrupt, autocratic government didn't seem worth defending. Atrocities like the 1968 My Lai Massacre of 347 Vietnamese civilians shook the public's faith in the project, while handing easy propaganda victories to America's opponents. After several years Americans broadly turned against Vietnam, and liberals led the charge.

During the 1968 election, Senator Eugene McCarthy challenged Lyndon Johnson from a nearly pacifist position, arguing not that the war couldn't be won, but that winning wasn't worth it: "I am concerned that the administration seems to have set no limits to the price that it is willing to pay for a military victory." McCarthy's campaign was disorganized and underfunded, but the resonance of his message was enough to convince LBJ to drop out of the race.

Four years later, another antiwar Democrat managed to win the nomination. Senator George McGovern had flown thirty-five bombing missions against the Nazis in a B-24. He couldn't be dismissed as a weakling afraid to draw blood. At the 1972 Democratic convention that summer, McGovern promised to withdraw the United States from Vietnam immediately: "[W]ithin ninety days of my inauguration, every American soldier and every American prisoner will be out of the jungle and out of their cells and then home in America where they belong."

The message failed. The McGovern campaign lost all but a single state in the general election to Richard Nixon. McGovern didn't reassess. If anything he hardened his position. Before leaving the race, McGovern made the case for what might now be described as an America First foreign policy: "This is also the time to turn away from excessive preoccupation overseas to the rebuilding of our own nation." It would be forty-four years before another presidential candidate made that point as forcefully, and he was a Republican.

Four years later, Jimmy Carter became the only antiwar Democrat to win the presidency, riding a wave of anti-incumbent rage after Watergate. For all his failings, Carter made good on his promise to keep U.S. troops out of harm's way. Depending on how you measure it, Carter may have been the only president in American history not to preside over a war. Only eight American servicemen died in action during his administration, killed accidentally during a failed attempt to rescue American hostages in Iran.

Politically, it didn't matter. Carter lost after only a term, drowned in the Reagan tsunami he helped create. Personally, Carter was an unappealing figure, sanctimonious and nasty. As an executive, he conveyed indecision and incompetence. Even his strengths looked like weakness. When Carter bragged about keeping America out of war, it seemed his real motive was self-doubt. He was hesitant to use force because he didn't trust American power.

Certainly many of his fellow liberals felt that way. Even at its peak, liberal antiwar rhetoric was never entirely coherent. Liberals didn't hate all wars, just those in which the United States projected its will abroad. Nobody ever said that out loud, but it was evident. Liberals were horrified by Nixon's bombing of Cambodia. They said nothing when the communist government of Vietnam invaded the same country a few years later. They complained about American military bases in Italy, but rarely mentioned the fact that Eastern Europe was occupied by Soviet troops. And of course, for pacifists, they seemed strangely attracted to Cuban leaders in military fatigues.

Liberals were never very consistent about where they stood on war, mostly because their positions were rooted in emotion rather than reason. But if their complaints about American imperialism were frequently childish, they nevertheless managed to make a couple of valid points.

The first is that war is destructive. It kills people. Wars flatten cities, hobble economies, topple civilizations, and upend ancient ways of doing things, often forever. In war, children always die.

None of this is hidden knowledge—nobody would deny that war destroys—but it's easy to forget it anyway. Look up any speech by a political leader ushering his country into conflict and you'll notice how nonspecific the descriptions are. It's always a battle for something abstract, like freedom or sovereignty. If politicians acknowledge that soldiers will be killed at all, it's only to extol their bravery and highlight the sheer glory of the endeavor. In speeches, war is never a bloody slog where eighteen-year-old boys get castrated by land mines, blasted apart by grenades, or pointlessly massacred in friendly-fire accidents, though that's exactly what it is.

Liberals reminded America of that. Yes, they were hysterical, inconsistent, and simplistic, and often motivated by a dislike of their own country. But on a basic level, they were right: war is not the answer; it's a means to an end, and a very costly one.

The second point that liberals made, often without knowing it, is that war is complicated. Once conflict starts, there's no predicting what will happen, or for how long. Violence tends to create chain reactions that move in unpredictable directions.

On an unexceptional June morning in 1914, a second-string Austrian nobleman was murdered by a Serbian terrorist in Sarajevo. In response, Austria prepared to attack Serbia. Russia in turn decided to defend Serbia, Germany supported its ally Austria, France supported Russia, Great Britain somehow became involved, and soon a small war over a single nobleman's death had sucked in every European great power.

Early on, commanders for both sides anticipated a short, triumphant conflict; the German kaiser told his men they would be home before the leaves fell from the trees. Instead, the continent was shredded by four years of mass killing. More than 16 million people died.

By the time World War I ended, four great empires with centuries-old monarchies had been destroyed. Wholly invented countries had risen in their place. Communism, previously a fringe ideology, held absolute control of Russia. Almost every significant conflict since, including World War II and the War on Terror, has its roots in what began that day in 1914. All the aftershocks of the death of a single minor nobleman, bleeding out in the streets of Sarajevo.

America has been granted no exception to the law of unintended consequences. In 1979, the Soviets invaded Afghanistan. Ronald Reagan came to power the next year pledging to do something about it, and soon did. By sending aid and weapons to the Afghan resistance, Reagan helped weaken the Russian position in Afghanistan, and ultimately the Soviet Union itself.

Democrats fought him on the policy from the beginning. Republicans accused liberals of being effectively pro-Soviet, and some of them were. Yet decades later you've got to wonder how wise it was to arm Muslim extremists waging a holy war in Southwest Asia. Both Osama bin Laden and Taliban founder Mohammed Omar got their first taste of warfare in the Afghan mujahideen.

Ironically, though, by the time it became clear that America had played a leading role in training its own enemies, liberals were in no position to complain. By that point, they were nearly as prowar as the Republicans.

The 1988 presidential campaign turned out to be the end of liberal pacifism. If you had to identify a moment of death, it would be the day the Dukakis campaign released video of its candidate riding in a tank with his helmet askew. An ad designed to show voters that Mike Dukakis wasn't a dopey peacenik had instead revealed the opposite: he was precisely that, an effete college professor type who didn't know which end of the gun the bullet came out of. Dukakis couldn't keep you safe. He probably didn't even want to. Within weeks, he blew a 17-point lead and lost to George H. W. Bush.

From the sidelines in Little Rock, Bill Clinton was watching carefully. Clinton was a lifelong peacenik himself, a Vietnam draft dodger who worked for the 1972 McGovern campaign, along with his wife, Hillary. But he wasn't stupid. He understood that Democrats kept losing in part because voters perceived them as weak. He vowed not to repeat the mistake.

In the middle of the 1992 New Hampshire primary campaign, when candidates were working twenty-hour days and not a minute was unscheduled, Clinton took a break to fly back to

Arkansas in order to preside over the lethal injection of a convicted murderer named Ricky Ray Rector. Rector was so profoundly brain damaged from a self-inflicted gunshot wound that it's not clear he knew he was about to die. After finishing his final meal, Rector asked the guards if he could save his dessert for later. Rival campaigns denounced the execution as inhumane. Clinton ignored them, and in November he won the general election.

The lesson was clear, and Clinton as president soon applied it to foreign policy. When he took office, Clinton inherited a several-thousand-troop humanitarian mission in Somalia, first deployed by President Bush. Clinton didn't simply continue the mission, he expanded it, deploying hundreds of U.S. Special Forces to battle Somali warlords. Clinton withdrew American forces only after nineteen U.S. troops were killed. Criticism came not from liberals in his own party, but from Republicans.

The experience was painful, but it did not halt future foreign interventions. In 1994, Clinton dispatched Marines to Haiti in order to topple the regime there. The following year, Clinton sent airpower to intervene in the Bosnian War. He later deployed more than sixteen thousand troops to the region. In 1999, the United States bombed Yugoslavia as part of the Kosovo War, and again, thousands of troops arrived as peacekeepers in the aftermath. Clinton sent cruise missiles into both Sudan and Afghanistan as well.

Clinton's most militant posture was reserved for Iraq, which the U.S. military bombed numerous times throughout his presidency. By the end of Clinton's second term, the United States was bombing Iraq an average of three times a week, at the cost of more than $1 billion a year.

After he left office, Clinton reflected that his main regret was that he hadn't been interventionist enough. He'd wanted to send American troops to Rwanda.

Politically, the decision to become a prowar party paid huge dividends for Democrats. From 1968 through 1988, Democrats decisively lost five presidential elections and narrowly won another. Since Clinton took the party back in a hawkish direction, the Democrats have lost the popular vote only once, in 2004.

For the country, however, there was a downside. With both parties aligned on the wisdom of frequent military intervention abroad, no one was left to make the counter case. As a result, America has remained in a state of almost permanent war.

One week after the World Trade Center fell, Congress voted to give President George W. Bush the authority to use military force against "nations, organizations, or persons he determines planned, authorized, committed, or aided the terrorist attacks that occurred on September 11, 2001." The law was utterly open-ended. There was no expiration date. No country or terror organization was mentioned by name. The president had congressional approval to do essentially whatever he wanted. Only a single member of Congress in either chamber voted against it, and she was a flake from Berkeley, California, an old antiwar liberal. Even her fellow Democrats mocked her.

There was now a bipartisan consensus on war, and it extended into the next conflict, Iraq. Indeed the predicate for that war had been laid by the previous administration, which hyped the threats of Saddam's weapons of mass destruction program.

"No one has done what Saddam Hussein has done, or is thinking of doing," Clinton's secretary of state Madeleine Albright told the audience at a town hall meeting at Ohio State University in 1998. "He is producing weapons of mass destruction, and he is qualitatively and quantitatively different from other dictators."

When some in the room expressed skepticism, Albright attacked their character. "I'm really surprised that people feel they need to defend the rights of Saddam Hussein," she said.

At least one person in the crowd wasn't intimidated. "You're not answering my question, Madame Albright," he yelled.

Albright's response: "As a former university professor, I suggest, sir, that you study carefully what American foreign policy is. Every one of the violations has been pointed out on what is not right, and I would be happy to spend fifty minutes with you after the forum to explain it."

She never did. Nor did Albright explain how exactly Saddam was "qualitatively and quantitatively" different from other strongmen around the world. She didn't need to. Everyone back in Washington already agreed with her.

In the fall of 2002, a total of seventy-seven senators voted in favor of the Iraq War resolution. This included the majority of Democrats, and 100 percent of the party's rising stars. Two future presidential candidates who voted for the war, John Kerry and Hillary Clinton, also happened to be future secretaries of state. The future vice president, Joe Biden, voted for it, as did the party's future vice presidential candidate, John Edwards. Future Senate leaders Harry Reid and Chuck Schumer supported the resolution, not to mention numerous future committee chairs like Dianne Feinstein. It was good politics for Democrats to support the war in Iraq, even within their own party.

Outside the Congress, relatively few mainstream liberals pushed back. Many aggressively supported the invasion. In 2002, the *New York Times* gave the case for war a sizable boost with a series of stories on Iraq's supposedly vibrant chemical and biological weapons programs. The articles cited anonymous Bush administration sources, who later went on television and cited the *Times* as evidence that what they had already told the paper on background was true. It was an airtight loop.

Strikingly, two of the *Times* reporters responsible for those stories had previously written books attacking Saddam Hussein. It's not a defense of the Iraqi regime to wonder how that might have affected their objectivity. Would the *New York Times* allow reporters who'd written books critical of abortion to cover the Supreme Court's reevaluation of *Roe v. Wade?* Probably not, though the hypothetical is absurd, since almost nobody at the paper opposes abortion.

In the end, the *Times* admitted the desire for war with Iraq clouded judgment in the newsroom. "Editors at several levels who should have been challenging reporters and pressing for more skepticism were perhaps too intent on rushing scoops into the paper," read the paper's postmortem. "Accounts of Iraqi defectors were not always weighed against their strong desire to have Saddam Hussein ousted."

It wasn't just the *Times*. Other establishment outlets did the same, including the *Washington Post* and the *Los Angeles Times*. Stories that confirmed the existence of Iraq's WMD program made the front page. Stories that raised doubts got buried. A postinvasion evaluation of coverage by the *New York Review of Books* concluded, "Despite abundant evidence of the administration's brazen misuse of intelligence . . . the press repeatedly let officials get away with it. As journalists rush to chronicle the administration's failings on Iraq, they should pay some attention to their own."

They did pay attention, at least for a while. While the initial invasion of Iraq toppled Saddam Hussein from power almost effortlessly, the war quickly became an expensive, bloody quagmire with no clear end objective in sight. U.S. casualties, initially low, spiraled into the thousands. Even worse, Iraq's WMD programs, the core justification for the war, proved to be illusory.

The many failures of the Iraq War triggered an Indian summer of antiwar sentiment on the left. In Connecticut, prowar senator Joe Lieberman lost his party's nomination in the Democratic primary to antiwar Ned Lamont (Lieberman held the seat running as an independent with strong Republican support). Michael Moore won an Oscar and became one of the left's intellectual leaders for his documentary *Fahrenheit 9/11,* which took a critical look not only at the Iraq War but the entire War on Terror. Cindy Sheehan, whose son was killed in Iraq, became a household name when she camped outside President Bush's Texas ranch demanding a personal meeting and an end to the war. Hundreds of thousands of people turned out for antiwar protests in Washington, D.C., and other major American cities.

But just as Indian summers eventually give way to winter, the revival of left-wing antiwar activism failed to reverse a long-term trend toward greater enthusiasm for war. When then-senator Barack Obama ran for president in 2008, he positioned himself as the antiwar candidate. He attacked his top opponent, Hillary Clinton, for supporting the 2002 war resolution and pledged to get U.S. troops out of Iraq.

But even this antiwar attitude was a pale shadow of the antiwar positions the left once adopted. McGovern had pledged peace in Vietnam within ninety days. Obama merely vowed to have U.S. combat troops out within sixteen months, and he counterbalanced that pledge with a promise to increase troop levels in Afghanistan.

Less than a year into his first term, Obama was awarded the Nobel Peace Prize, apparently for the transcendent achievement of not being George W. Bush. But the prize had no lasting effect on Obama. Under his stewardship the Democratic establishment once again became a party of war, differing from Republicans only on exactly how much war they wanted, and where.

In 2011, Hillary Clinton and other interventionists in the administration convinced Obama to support the overthrow of Muammar Gaddafi in Libya. It was never obvious why Gaddafi needed to be killed. While he'd once supported terrorist efforts against the West and established nuclear and chemical weapons programs, his behavior had dramatically improved following the invasion of Iraq. He shuttered his WMD programs in December 2003, was removed from America's list of state terror sponsors, and even collaborated with the European Union to block illegal migration from Africa into Europe.

Gaddafi was an unsavory autocrat. But there were far more dangerous and more repressive regimes out there, and there was no clear replacement for him within Libya. If there's a single lesson of the Iraq War, it's that chaos is worse than dictatorship. Libya looked like a prime candidate for chaos. With Gaddafi gone, it was obvious that the place might devolve into a lawless mess and become a bug light for extremist groups.

Hillary Clinton and Samantha Power of the National Security Council didn't agree. They viewed Gaddafi as a deeply immoral man. That's all the justification they needed to take him out. So they did. With Gaddafi on the brink of victory in the Libyan civil war, the United States and its NATO allies intervened, taking over the country's airspace, bombing Gaddafi's forces, and turning the tide of the conflict. Seven months later, Gaddafi was toppled from power, captured, and unceremoniously killed.

The establishment applauded. Obama's overthrow of the Gaddafi government, declared the *New York Times*, was "an historic victory for the people of Libya who, with NATO's help, transformed their country from an international pariah into a nation with the potential to become a productive partner with the West."

The triumphant tone evokes another famous *Times* dispatch, from Cambodia in April 1975. The headline: "Indochina Without Americans: For Most, a Better Life." That story ran in the paper four days before the Khmer Rouge entered Phnom Penh and began murdering more than a third of the country's population.

The aftermath in Libya hasn't been quite as bloody, but that's small comfort. Instead of creating a democratic, Westernized Libya, Obama's destruction of Gaddafi simply created a new failed state. Rather than marginalizing radical Islam, Gaddafi's fall empowered it, and by 2014 the country was in another civil war that killed thousands. ISIS militants have found a haven in the lawless country. While Gaddafi had blocked illegal migration to Europe, the new Libya has been powerless to stop it, and hundreds of thousands of African migrants have made their way to Europe from Libyan ports.

Things got so bad in Libya after Gaddafi was deposed that even the *Times* had to acknowledge it might be some time before the country could become "a productive partner with the

West." Luckily, the *Times* had a solution: more American intervention in Libya.

Remarkably, an editorial in August 2016 cited the very same 2011 disaster the paper once endorsed as a justification for repeating the same mistake: "The United States demonstrated during its involvement in the 2011 civil war that led to the ouster of Col. Muammar el-Qaddafi that American airstrikes can change battlefield fortunes."

In Washington, military action is assumed to be preferable to inaction, regardless of outcome. Barack Obama—who campaigned for president on the promise to withdraw from Iraq—not only bombed the country, the fourth American president in a row to do so, but by the end of his term had recommitted troops on the ground. Republicans didn't seem to find this odd. Their main complaint was that he sent too few.

Liberals, meanwhile, stood by (and in some cases cheered) as Obama expanded the War on Terror beyond the boundaries of the Bush years. After two terms, Obama had ordered the killing of nearly four thousand people by drone attacks, most of them in "non-battlefield" areas like Yemen, Somalia, and Pakistan. Some of the people killed were American citizens, struck down as "enemy combatants" despite being far away from U.S. troops, in countries the United States was not at war with.

By 2013, the lessons of Iraq and Libya still unlearned, Obama was preparing for another regime change, this time in Syria. The cycle was eerily similar. Syrian president Bashar Assad was undoubtedly a cruel, authoritarian figure, but he also was not a clear threat to the United States, and it was impossible to know who might replace him should he fall. Nevertheless, following a chemical attack on civilians during the country's civil war, Secretary of State John Kerry gave an impassioned speech about Assad's human rights abuses and argued that a military intervention was needed. A now-familiar cycle began again.

The *New York Times* was back with its full support. In an editorial, the paper noted that "it would be highly unlikely—if not irresponsible—for [President Obama] to authorize Mr. Kerry to speak in such sweeping terms and then do nothing." The next day, the *Times* ran an opinion piece titled "Bomb Syria, Even if It's Illegal."

Strong popular opposition ultimately scuttled Obama's plans to bomb Assad's government, though seven out of the ten senators who voted for it were Democrats. But it was only a temporary reprieve. Removing Assad from power remained the official policy of the U.S. government. By the end of the Obama years, America was not only bombing Syria but had ground troops there, this time for the purposes of fighting the Islamic State.

And not just there, but a number of other places as well. On Election Day 2016, after eight years of rule by the nominally "antiwar" faction of U.S. politics, American troops were stationed on roughly eight hundred military bases in seventy nations. The Pentagon was dropping bombs on at least seven different countries. Barack Obama was the first president to serve two full terms, and preside over war for every single day of them.

Not all of that was Obama's choosing. He didn't start the wars in Iraq or Afghanistan. But he didn't pull back much, either. What's particularly striking, however, is how little Democrats said about it. Apart from some rumblings from the far left, there were no protests in the streets. In 2008, three antiwar documentaries were nominated for Best Documentary at the Academy Awards, and Hollywood stars routinely bashed President

Bush's foreign policy. On January 21, that all evaporated. Popular culture seemed oblivious.

In 2016 there wasn't a single antiwar song in the top 100 pop hits.

———

Liberals were no longer interested in giving peace a chance. If anything, by the 2016 presidential election, liberals seemed most agitated by the idea of not being in conflict with other countries. In one of those weird historical ironies that almost nobody seemed to appreciate at the time, the Republican in the race was running well to the left of his Democratic opponent on key foreign policy questions. Donald Trump gave speech after speech attacking the wars in Iraq and Afghanistan, and the idea of nation building more broadly. Hillary Clinton was still defending the decision to kill Gaddafi.

Nowhere was the divide broader or more bewildering than on Russia. Trump argued it would be in America's interest to make common cause with the Russian government when possible, especially in the fight against Islamic extremism. Liberals, who for decades defended Russia when it was run by the Soviets, dismissed the idea out of hand as irresponsible, possibly even unpatriotic.

Yet again, the *New York Times* led the way. Two days before the 2016 GOP convention in Cleveland, the *Times* announced that "decades after the end of the Cold War, Moscow, led now by the ambitious, aggressive and unpredictable Vladimir Putin, has returned as a major threat."

The paper would spend the better part of the next year detailing that threat and implicitly suggesting that it deserved a military response. Less than a week after the election, the *Times* editorial board warned of "the dangers of going soft on Russia." The paper repeatedly described the hacking of the Democratic National Committee's email servers as an "act of war" by Vladimir Putin. Democrats in Congress and on cable news repeated the charge.

Were they serious, or just baiting Trump? Both probably, but more the former than you might expect. At the end of March 2017, the administration indicated it would be ending the Obama-era policy of seeking regime change in Syria. "Our priority is no longer to sit and focus on getting Assad out," explained U.S. ambassador to the United Nations Nikki Haley.

The foreign policy establishment responded with outrage. Figures from both parties described the policy change as a concession to Russia, a major backer of the Assad regime, and therefore as a betrayal of the United States.

Five days later, U.S. intelligence agencies announced that the Assad government had dropped chemical weapons on civilians in northern Syria, killing at least twenty children. No one doubted Assad was capable of committing atrocities, but this one seemed counterproductive, to put it mildly. Indeed it was one of the few things Assad could have done to reverse U.S. policy on removing him from office. Essentially it was the most effective way to sabotage his all-but-assured victory in the Syrian civil war. According to American officials, he did it anyway.

It didn't make sense. Why would a man as canny and resilient as Bashar Assad do something so pointless and self-destructive? Apparently, because he was so innately evil, he couldn't help himself. That was the explanation from self-described Syria experts in Washington, few of whom could speak Arabic or had ever lived in Syria. Bad people do bad things. Assad is bad. He must go.

Within days, the Trump administration caved to the pressure and lobbed missiles into Syria. There were a lot of questions about the move, beginning with: What was the point? If we took out Assad, who would replace him? And by the way, how did we know for certain the Syrian government ordered the chemical attack? Didn't the Syrian rebels have chemical weapons, too? Couldn't the decision have been the work of underlings rather than top commanders?

For the most part, questions like these went unasked. Instead, for the first time since Trump received the GOP nomination, elites in both parties cheered. The media congratulated the new president for his courage and steadfast leadership. According to a Harvard study, the Syrian missile strike was the only decision Trump made in his first one hundred days that received positive press coverage.

Even Trump's opponents in Congress loved it. Senator Chuck Schumer, leader of the Senate Democrats, described the attack as "the right thing to do." The senior Democrat in the House, Nancy Pelosi, called it a "proportional response." Senators Dick Durbin and Elizabeth Warren agreed. Former House majority leader Steny Hoyer said his only complaint was that Trump didn't go far enough.

For the first time in memory, Democrats in Washington were every bit as hawkish as Republicans. The alignment was complete. How did that happen?

The first step for Democrats was embracing violence as a tool of positive social change. In 1965, liberals viewed the bombing of North Vietnam as a moral atrocity. Thirty years later, they applauded Bill Clinton's bombing of Bosnia as a means of protecting the rights of a vulnerable minority group, the local Muslim population. Liberals discovered that war was an expedient form of social engineering, not to mention politically popular. Want to save children? Bomb their country. Head Start suddenly seemed like a tepid half measure compared to the swift compassion of air strikes.

How often do bombings actually improve people's lives? Do children on the ground really like them? Who knows? Follow-up stories on the aftermath of cruise missile attacks are notably rare in American media.

The practical effects of the policies are less interesting to policy makers in Washington than the spirit in which they're intended. When you're pulling the trigger, the spirit is always pure. Liberals believed that Curtis LeMay dropped bombs because he was a crazed warmonger who took pleasure in hurting people. Liberals believe they bomb countries for the same reason they once opposed bombing countries, because they want to make the world a better place. Intent is what matters.

The second force driving the shift was a change in leadership in America's biggest institutions. Liberal skepticism of the Vietnam War was inseparable from a generalized suspicion of the establishment. The left distrusted the government's rhetoric and goals in the Vietnam War because the left distrusted the government itself. Liberals knew powerful people were happy to lie to them.

Liberals now control those elite institutions. They no longer distrust power; they wield it.

We were better off with Curtis LeMay. When moral certainty meets indifference to detail, anything can happen. You can overthrow a secular dictator, watch as he's replaced by bloodthirsty religious nuts who make everything worse, and then attempt the very same thing somewhere else, expecting different results. And never feel bad about it.

It's amusing to think that well-educated professionals once considered Lyndon Johnson the world's greatest threat to peace. What they hated most about Johnson was his naked cynicism. That was appalling, but it was far from the worst thing.

The most dangerous force of all turns out to be an activist establishment that believes its heart is in the right place.

——

The signature characteristic of America's foreign policy establishment, apart from their foolishness, is the resiliency of their self-esteem. No matter how often they're wrong, no matter how many disasters they unintentionally create, they never seem to feel bad about it. They certainly never blame themselves. Part of the reason for this is that most of them live in Washington.

Washington isn't like everywhere else. The city's economy is tied directly to the size of the federal budget, which has grown virtually without pause since the attack on Pearl Harbor in 1941. The District of Columbia and its surrounding suburbs are now the wealthiest metro region in the country.

Washington's job market is effectively bulletproof. Political figures cycle in and out of government, from lobbying to finance to contracting and back, growing richer at every turn. In Washington, prosperity is all but guaranteed.

To the rest of the country, this looks like corruption, because, essentially, it is. But if you live there, it's all upside.

The most interesting effect of uninterrupted economic growth is that the culture of the city remains unusually stable.

Even as Washington's population has grown exponentially over the years, many things about the city haven't changed at all. Most of the affluent neighborhoods look the same demographically as they did in 1960. Mothers don't work. Divorce is unusual. Housing prices almost never fall. It's a cultural time capsule.

By voter registration, D.C. is the most Democratic city in America. Yet the instincts of the people who live there are deeply conservative. Washingtonians hate change.

More than anything, they hate to be told they're wrong, or their ideas are stupid, especially when they are. This explains much of official Washington's hostility to Donald Trump.

It is possible to isolate the precise moment that Trump permanently alienated the Republican establishment in Washington: February 13, 2016. There was a GOP primary debate that night in Greenville, South Carolina, so every Republican in Washington was watching. Seemingly out of nowhere, Trump articulated something that no party leader had ever said out loud. "We should never have been in Iraq," Trump announced, his voice rising. "We have destabilized the Middle East."

Many in the crowd booed, but Trump kept going: "They lied. They said there were weapons of mass destruction. There were none. And they knew there were none."

Pandemonium seemed to erupt in the hall, and on television. Shocked political analysts declared that the Trump presidential effort had just euthanized itself. Republican voters, they said with certainty, would never accept attacks on policies their party had espoused and carried out.

Back in Washington, rival GOP campaigns frantically searched for ways to discredit what Trump had said. They found what they considered a silver bullet in a recording of an episode of the Howard Stern radio show from 2002, in which Trump seemed to approve of the idea of overthrowing Saddam.

By Washington standards, this qualified as a kill shot. The candidate had once uttered complimentary words about a war that had not yet started. Therefore, he had no right to criticize the same war fourteen years later, after it had proved disastrous. Consultants for the Jeb! and Marco Rubio campaigns traded high fives.

Republican voters had a different reaction. They understood that adults sometimes change their minds based on evidence. They themselves had come to understand that the Iraq War was a mistake. They appreciated hearing something verboten but true.

Rival Republicans denounced Trump as an apostate. Voters considered him brave.

Trump won the South Carolina primary, and shortly after that, the Republican nomination.

Republicans in Washington never recovered. When Trump attacked the Iraq War and questioned the integrity of the people who planned and promoted it, he was attacking them. They hated him for that.

Some of them became so angry, it distorted their judgment and character.

———

Bill Kristol is probably the most influential Republican strategist of the post-Reagan era. Born in 1954, Kristol was the second child of the writer Irving Kristol, one of the founders of neoconservatism. Like most early neoconservatives, Irving Kristol was a former leftist, a childhood Trotskyite who became progressively disillusioned with failures of government social policy, and with the left's infatuation with the Soviet Union.

The neoconservatism of Irving Kristol and his friends was jarring to the ossified liberal establishment of the time, but in retrospect it was basically a centrist philosophy: pragmatic, tolerant of a limited welfare state, not rigidly ideological. By the time Bill Kristol got done with it forty years later, neoconservatism was something else entirely.

Kristol came to Washington in the mid-1980s to work for the Reagan administration, after several years of teaching at Harvard. In 1995, he founded the *Weekly Standard*. I joined the *Standard* as a reporter that year, about a month before the magazine launched, and stayed until early 2001. Kristol was in his prime. The publication was explicitly conservative, but most of the time the writers could write what they wanted. I found Kristol a humane and decent boss, if a little cold. He was funny as hell in meetings.

What I didn't understand at the time was that Kristol had an unstated agenda that informed much of what the *Weekly Standard* did. The writers in the office thought we were engaged in conservative journalism. Kristol was trying to remake the Republican Party.

Years later, writer Philip Weiss described a conversation he had with Kristol in which this became explicit. There are Republicans, Kristol told Weiss, "of whom I disapprove so much that I won't appear with them. That I've encouraged that they be expelled or not welcomed into the Republican Party. I'd be happy if Ron Paul left and ran as a third party candidate. I was very happy when Pat Buchanan was allowed to go off and run as a third party candidate."

Unbeknownst to his staff, Bill Kristol had no intention of being merely a magazine publisher, or a disseminator of conservative ideas. He saw himself as the ideological gatekeeper of the Republican Party.

I wish I'd known this when I worked there. Kristol was always encouraging me to write hit pieces on Pat Buchanan, and on a couple of occasions I did. At the time I had no idea this was part of a larger strategy, though it did strike me as a little odd. In one of those coincidences that happen regularly in a city as small as Washington, Pat Buchanan's sister Kathleen was Kristol's assistant at the *Standard*, and well liked by everyone. Buchanan himself was an appealing guy personally, beloved by the people around him. And his politics weren't entirely crazy. A lot of what Buchanan predicted in the 1990s turned out to be true.

The animus wasn't personal. Kristol got along with Buchanan when they saw each other. Kristol didn't even disagree with most of Buchanan's views on social questions. In private, Kristol was as witheringly antigay as Buchanan was in public. The disagreement was entirely over foreign policy.

At his core, that's what Kristol cared about. That's why he despised figures as seemingly disconnected as Pat Buchanan and Ron Paul. One of the few things Paul and Buchanan had in common was opposition to more war in the Middle East. Kristol believed the United States should be bombing and invading countries throughout the region.

Almost from the moment Operation Desert Storm concluded in 1991, Kristol began pushing for the overthrow of Saddam Hussein. In 1997, the *Standard* ran a cover story titled "Saddam Must Go." If the United States didn't launch a ground invasion of Iraq, the lead editorial warned, the world should "get ready for the day when Saddam has biological and chemical weapons at the tips of missiles aimed at Israel and at American forces in the Gulf."

In 1998, Kristol, along with Donald Rumsfeld and Robert Kagan, signed a letter to Clinton calling for "removing Saddam Hussein and his regime from power."

That same year, as the Clinton administration planned air raids on Iraq, Kristol and Kagan made their case for regime change. "Unless we act" in Iraq, they warned in a *New York Times* op-ed, "the Middle East will be destabilized . . . and American soldiers will have to pay a far heavier price when the international peace sustained by American leadership begins to collapse."

Around this time, Bob Kagan became a fixture in the *Weekly Standard* offices. Kagan always struck me as very much like Kristol, in that both were products of academia and had similar views on the world. The main difference was that Kagan was dumber and less charming. Kristol came off as erudite and urbane. Those were his basic strengths. Kagan, who like Kristol had a graduate degree from Harvard, seemed like an aging linebacker with a history of concussions. Rather than make his case during conversations in the office, Kagan just increased his volume. When challenged, he yelled and stormed off. I always thought Kagan was an idiot. Not that it slowed him down as a foreign policy expert in Washington.

After the September 11 attacks, Kristol found a new opening to start a war with Iraq. He started pushing immediately. On September 12, 2001, as downtown New York smoldered, Kristol told NPR, "I think Iraq is, actually, the big unspoken elephant in the room today." In another NPR appearance the next month, he said, "We know that over the last three or four weeks, [Saddam] has moved many of his chemical and biological weapons programs in preparation for possible U.S. attacks."

In November 2001, Kristol and Kagan wrote a piece in the *Weekly Standard* alleging that Saddam Hussein hosted a training camp for Al Qaeda fighters where terrorists had trained to hijack planes. They suggested that Mohammad Atta, mastermind of the 9/11 attacks, was actively collaborating with Saddam's intelligence services. On the basis of no evidence, they accused Iraq of fomenting the anthrax attacks on American politicians and news outlets.

"What will it take for the FBI and the CIA to start connecting the dots here?" Kristol and Kagan asked. "A signed confession from Saddam?" That confession never came. No evidence was ever found tying Iraq to the 9/11 attacks.

Many people believed Kristol's claims. In the first couple of years after 9/11, it seemed like just about anything could be true. But even policy makers sympathetic to the idea of overthrowing the Iraqi government and occupying the country found themselves worrying about the aftermath. Saddam goes, but what then?

Kristol had no such concerns. He mocked those who did. "If we want to be popular in the Arab world, we should liberate the people of Iraq from Saddam," he said during a Fox News appearance in April 2002. In November 2002, he predicted that removing Saddam would have a positive "chain reaction" effect across the Middle East. The following February, he declared that "if we free the people of Iraq, we will be respected in the Arab world . . . and I think we will be respected around the world."

In March 2003, twelve years of advocacy paid off. America attacked Iraq. Kristol was quick to boast about his triumph. As U.S. troops entered the country, Kristol told C-SPAN, "This is going to be a two-month war, not an eight-year war."

To those concerned about the possibility of ethnic conflict within Iraq, Kristol waved his hand. "There has been a certain amount of pop sociology," he explained a month after the invasion, "that the Shi'a can't get along with the Sunni. There's almost no evidence of that at all."

It's a measure of how little experts in Washington actually know that Kristol kept getting invited to speak as an authority on the Middle East. No evidence the Shia and Sunnis might fight each other in Iraq? Your average Arab cabdriver would laugh at that claim. It's ridiculous. The Iraqi regime was repressive largely because it's so difficult to govern a country riven by religious factionalism, as modern Iraq has always been. Everyone who's been to the region knows that. Apparently nobody told Bill Kristol.

Time has proved Kristol spectacularly wrong on Iraq, on the big questions as well as the specifics. He has never acknowledged that, much less apologized. He's too implicated.

"I'm not apologizing for something that I think was not wrong," Kristol said in 2014. "The war to remove Saddam was the right thing and necessary thing to do."

Two years later, he seemed even more disconnected from reality. "The war in Iraq was right and necessary, and we won it," Kristol said. At the time, Mosul, once Iraq's second-largest city, was under the control of the Islamic State. Iraq was embroiled in a civil war that would kill at least ninety thousand people.

Because Kristol has refused to learn from the failures he

helped create, his foreign policy positions have remained un-changed for more than twenty-five years, even as the world has changed completely. To almost every problem, Kristol's solution remains the same: war, led by America.

In the summer of 2006, Kristol demanded regime change in both Syria and Iran, in response to fighting between Israel and Hezbollah in Lebanon. According to Kristol, taking out the leadership of both countries, while basically irrelevant to core U.S. interests, was somehow "our war." Indeed, Kristol ex-plained, Hezbollah's attacks on Israel were America's fault. "We have been too weak, and have allowed ourselves to be perceived as weak," he said.

To atone for its weakness, Kristol argued, America should commence air strikes against the Iranian regime immediately. "It would be easier to act sooner rather than later," he wrote, without explaining why it was necessary for America to act at all. "Yes, there would be repercussions—and they would be healthy ones, showing a strong America that has rejected further ap-peasement."

Kristol's demands for war in the Middle East continued throughout the Obama administration. In 2011, he backed in-tervention in Libya, including with American ground troops. In 2013, he demanded intervention in Syria to topple Assad. In 2014, he called for a reinvasion of Iraq to defeat the Islamic State.

Under ordinary circumstances, Bill Kristol would be famous for being wrong. Kristol still goes on television regularly, but it's not to apologize for the many demonstrably untrue things he's said about the Middle East, or even to talk about foreign pol-icy. Instead, Kristol goes on TV to attack Donald Trump. In a remarkable late-life conversion, Kristol has become one of the most passionate critics of the Trump administration.

Tellingly, it didn't begin like this. Kristol once defended Trump. In June 2015, just weeks after Trump announced for president, Kristol urged the other candidates in the race to listen carefully to what Trump was saying. Some of his rhetoric, Kristol said, resonated with voters, and for good reason:

> Trump understands that Americans like winning: "Our country is in serious trouble. We don't have victories any-more. We used to have victories, but we don't have them." Trump is aware the public believes international politics is more zero-sum than globalist elites like to think. "Our en-emies are getting stronger and stronger, by the way, and we as a country are getting weaker." So Trump is pro-tough-trade-negotiations, he's pro-China-bashing, and he's pro-military. "I will find within our military, I will find the General Patton or I will find General MacArthur, I will find the right guy. I will find the guy that's going to take that military and make it really work. Nobody, nobody will be pushing us around." A bit simple-minded? Sure. Closer to the truth than the cocktail partiers at Davos? Probably. Closer in sentiment to the American people? Certainly.

The qualified praise continued for months. Kristol fre-quently had more good things than bad to say about Donald Trump. He criticized Trump's opponents for not bothering to understand his appeal.

"I remain not pro-Trump, but I'm once again drifting into the anti-anti-Trump camp," Kristol wrote in August 2015. "Much of the criticism of Trump has the feel of falling (fairly or unfairly) into the hobgoblin-of-small-minds category."

Then came the South Carolina primary debate. Trump criticized the Iraq War and its promoters. Kristol erupted. He was as angry as he had ever been in public about anything. Kristol denounced not just Trump, but anyone who didn't join him in denouncing Trump.

"Once upon a time we had leaders who would have expressed their outrage at such a slander," he wrote in the *Weekly Standard*. "They would have explained to the American people how extraordinarily irresponsible his slander was, and would have done their best to discredit a man who could behave so irresponsibly. They would have pronounced him unfit to be president of the United States, and they would have mobilized their friends, supporters and admirers to ensure so appalling an eventuality didn't come to pass."

Suddenly Kristol found himself aligned with the cocktail partiers at Davos he once mocked. Global elites might oppose the interests of American voters, but at least they didn't accuse Bill Kristol of lying about Iraq. Kristol lapsed into a kind of public nervous breakdown, once coming close to tears on television, as he tried to stop Trump.

He failed. Trump won the nomination, but Kristol barely took a breath. He began searching for a warm body willing to mount a third-party challenge that would guarantee Hillary Clinton's victory in the general election.

Kristol had lunch with Mitt Romney in Washington to discuss a third-party run. He encouraged Senators Tom Cotton and Marco Rubio to jump into the race, as well as General James Mattis. When all of them declined, Kristol settled on a little-known writer for *National Review* named David French.

French seemed nice enough but clearly didn't fully understand what he was getting into.

Kristol tried to pressure French into running by preemptively announcing his candidacy. In May 2016, Kristol tweeted, "There will be an independent candidate—an impressive one, with a strong team and a real chance."

Apparently this scared French. Within days he announced he wasn't running. Few voters noticed.

Eventually, Kristol drafted a congressional staffer and former CIA employee named Evan McMullin. Like French, McMullin was new to public life, all but unknown outside his immediate circle of acquaintances. But McMullin had two qualities essential for the job Kristol had in mind: unusually high self-regard, and a willingness to defend the Iraq War. McMullin entered the race. He finished in November with less than 1 percent of the vote.

Trump's election seemed to undo Bill Kristol entirely. He lost his job at the *Weekly Standard* after more than twenty years, forced out by owners who were panicked about declining readership. He seemed to spend most of his time on Twitter ranting about Trump.

Before long he was ranting about the people who elected Trump. At an American Enterprise Institute panel event in February 2017, Kristol made the case for why immigrants are more impressive than native-born Americans. "Basically if you are in free society, a capitalist society, after two, three, four generations of hard work, everyone becomes kind of decadent, lazy, spoiled, whatever." Most Americans, Kristol said, "grew up as spoiled kids and so forth."

A year later, Kristol had moved even further. In February 2018, Kristol tweeted that he would "take in a heartbeat a group of newly naturalized American citizens over the spoiled native-born know-nothings" who supported Trump.

By the spring of 2018, Kristol was considering a run for president himself. He was still making the case for the invasion of Iraq, as well as pushing for a new war, this time in Syria, and maybe in Lebanon and Iran, too. Like most people in Washington, he'd learned nothing at all.

FOUR

Shut Up, They Explained

I f you're going to run a country for the benefit of a few, it's dangerous to let people complain about it. The only way to impose unpopular policies on a population is through fear and silence. Free speech is the enemy of authoritarian rule. That's why the Framers put it at the top of the Bill of Rights. That's also why our ruling class seeks to crush it.

Not that any ruling class has ever supported free speech for long. In the summer of 1917, a Socialist Party official in Philadelphia named Charles Schenck spent $150 to have fifteen thousand political pamphlets printed. The United States had entered the war in Europe that spring, and Schenck was hoping to convince draft-age men not to serve.

"When you conscript a man and compel him to go abroad and fight against his will," the tract argued, "you violate the most sacred right of personal liberty," as protected by the Thirteenth Amendment. "Exercise your rights of free speech." The headline over Schenck's essay read: "Long Live the Constitution of the United States."

A judge promptly issued a warrant for Schenck's arrest. Federal agents raided his office, seized his pamphlets, and carted Schenck off to jail. Charged under the recently passed Espionage Act, he was convicted on three counts and sent to federal prison.

It's hard to believe an American citizen could be jailed for expressing a political opinion, but it was common at the time. Schenck was one of thousands of Americans prosecuted by the Wilson administration for disagreeing with its policies. Remarkably, this did not seem to strike most Americans as strange or unconstitutional. Charles Schenck did not become a folk hero. His appeal, when it finally arrived at the Supreme Court, was unanimously denied. He died in obscurity.

Only radicals cared about what had happened to Charles Schenck. The American Civil Liberties Union was formed in 1920 in part as a reaction to his case and others like it. For decades after its founding, the ACLU took an absolutist position on the First Amendment: ACLU lawyers defended free speech in all cases, and with particular vigor when that speech was unpopular or outright despised.

It sometimes seemed like there wasn't a villain or miscreant the ACLU wasn't eager to represent. Klansmen, communists, anti-Semites, pornographers—all got free legal counsel when the ACLU determined their right to speak was under attack.

When a Denver theater owner was arrested for screening D. W. Griffith's film *The Birth of a Nation* (a local ordinance banned movies that incited "race hatred"), the ACLU defended him. When the U.S. Post Office burned copies of James Joyce's unreadable modernist novel *Ulysses* on obscenity grounds, the ACLU took the case to court. Militant atheists got help from the ACLU. So did any number of draft dodgers, as well as Jehovah's Witnesses who refused to salute the flag.

Maybe the most reviled client the ACLU ever took was an American Nazi leader named Frank Collin. In 1977, Collin and a small group of self-styled fascists applied for a permit to march through the Chicago suburb of Skokie, Illinois. More than half of Skokie's residents were Jewish; several thousand had survived Nazi concentration camps. The Nazis had chosen the venue to cause maximum outrage, and they succeeded. The town of Skokie denied the permit; an Illinois judge later ratified that decision. The ACLU took the case.

Everything about the ACLU's position was offensive. Not only were its lawyers defending the National Socialist Party of America, but Frank Collin himself was cartoonishly repulsive, even by the standards of Nazis. He looked and dressed like Adolf Hitler, complete with a brown shirt, swastika armband, and greasy bangs. Collin later turned out to be half-Jewish himself; his own father had been held at Dachau. Not long after Skokie, Collin went to prison for molesting boys.

The ACLU represented Frank Collin all the way through the federal court system. Thousands of ACLU members quit in disgust. Many others withheld financial support. Some complained that not only did the ACLU defend Nazis, they'd sent a Jewish lawyer to do it. It was too much, even for fervent supporters of free speech.

You can see why. How could a decent person voluntarily

represent Nazis? It was horrifying, but also revealing. You'd really have to believe in free speech to represent someone whose speech you despised, especially if it meant losing donors and being criticized by your neighbors.

The ACLU really believed in free speech. Their dedication succeeded. In a 5–4 decision, the Supreme Court ruled that even publicly marching with the swastika was protected speech.

There was a time when the First Amendment qualified as secular scripture for educated Americans. They might abhor your views, but they'd die for your right to express them. That's what they always said, and there was clearly truth in it. Freedom of speech was vital not just because it's inherently gratifying to say what you think, but because speech is the foundational right of an open society. Free speech makes free thought possible. All other rights derive from it. The right to express your views is the final bulwark that shields the individual from the mob that disagrees with him. Without freedom of speech, we are not free.

Interpretations of the First Amendment evolved over time, and for decades the ACLU looked for vehicles to expand them. In the summer of 1964, they found an unlikely one. Clarence Brandenburg was a small-time Ku Klux Klan leader from western Ohio. In August of that year, he invited a Cincinnati TV station to film a rally consisting of about a dozen Klansmen. With cameras rolling, the group burned a cross, and Brandenburg gave a speech attacking blacks and Jews. "We're not a revengent [sic] organization," he said, "but if our president, our Congress, our Supreme Court, continues to suppress the white, Caucasian race, it's possible that there might have to be some revengeance [sic] taken."

Police arrested Brandenburg for his words. An Ohio court convicted him of violating a state law that banned the promotion of "crime, sabotage, violence or unlawful methods of terrorism" for political ends, and sent him to jail. The ACLU took up his appeal.

Five years later, the Supreme Court ruled unanimously that Clarence Brandenburg had a constitutional right to say what he did. The justices concluded that government could not limit expression except in cases where speech "is directed to inciting or producing imminent lawless action," and is likely to produce such action.

Convincing rioters to torch a bank was prohibited. Calling for revolution (or in Brandenburg's words, "revengeance") was not. In the opinion of Justice William O. Douglas, "government has no power to invade [the] sanctuary of belief and conscience."

In practice, the *Brandenburg v. Ohio* decision allowed nearly every form of speech, no matter how odious. If threats from a robed Klansman ranting in front of a burning cross were constitutionally protected, all opinions are. Americans could say pretty much anything they wanted without fear of legal reprisal. Writers and intellectuals celebrated the decision as a critical victory for freedom and the rights of all Americans.

In retrospect, this was the high-water mark of American liberalism. Attitudes about speech began to change shortly thereafter, though as late as the 1990s you still heard old hippies describe the First Amendment as America's greatest achievement. Lots of places have market economies and democratic forms of government. Only the United States has the guarantee of free expression. Almost every other country prosecutes its citizens for having unpopular views, even peaceful Canada. We don't. It's what sets America apart. This isn't just a free country, it's the freest.

Radicals cared about the First Amendment because they knew they benefited from its protections. Freedom of speech doesn't exist for the sake of those in power. It exists to safeguard the rights of the unpopular and out of step. Martin Luther King was jailed for leading protests against segregation. Hundreds of suspected communists were blacklisted in Hollywood. People were fired from jobs for their beliefs. Radicals knew free speech mattered. When you're in the despised minority, being able to say what you think is the only real power you have.

The opposite is also true. There's nothing more infuriating to a ruling class than contrary opinions. They're inconvenient and annoying. They're evidence of an ungrateful population. They impede the progress of your programs. Above all, they constitute a threat to your authority; disagreement is the first step toward insurrection. When you're in charge, you'll do what you can to suppress dissent.

The modern establishment has done exactly that. Once they took over the institutions they formerly opposed, liberals abandoned their historic support for the First Amendment and became its enemies. Nowhere was the change more profound or perverse than at the University of California, Berkeley, birthplace of the Free Speech Movement.

In 1964, a graduate student at Berkeley named Jack Weinberg set up a table on campus and began passing out unauthorized political literature. He was promptly arrested and thrown into a patrol car. Thousands of students surrounded the vehicle and prevented it from moving for more than a day. Joan Baez arrived to sing ballads of encouragement. Many hundreds of protesters were arrested, but in the end Weinberg was released. School administrators caved to student demands for free expression. Berkeley's campus became synonymous with unfettered speech.

It remained that way for the next fifty years.

———

By the winter of 2017, when writer Milo Yiannopoulos arrived to speak, Berkeley had become the mirror image of its former self. Students were still willing to commit acts of civil disobedience, but this time they protested in order to silence a speaker. Activists at Berkeley accused Yiannopoulos of being a "racist, misogynistic demagogue" who "notoriously riles up a lynch-mob mentality in his audiences" with the aim of "promoting violence."

Jesse Arreguin, the mayor of Berkeley, agreed with the students. "Using speech to silence marginalized communities and promote bigotry is unacceptable," Arreguin tweeted hours before the scheduled start of Yiannopoulos's event. "Hate speech isn't welcome in our community."

In order to show their disapproval of hate and violence, Berkeley students rioted. Protesters lit fires, smashed windows, and threw rocks, committing at least one hundred thousand dollars in property damage. Six people were injured, including a woman who had come to see Yiannopoulos speak. She was pepper-sprayed in the face while giving an interview to a local news crew. Local police, ordered by the city to do nothing, refused to act. Yiannopoulos fled for his safety with security guards in an unmarked car. He never gave his speech.

A few months later, at a forum on "progressive mayorships," Jesse Arreguin argued that people like Milo Yiannopoulos shouldn't be allowed to speak in public. "Public safety is our top priority," he explained. "And that actually, I believe, takes precedence over freedom of speech."

It wasn't just Berkeley where Yiannopoulos found himself under attack. At DePaul University in 2016, a College Republicans event featuring Yiannopoulos was shut down when students stormed the stage and seized his microphone. Campus security staff did nothing to intervene or restore order. Afterward, school administrators released a statement affirming the value of free speech, but they didn't mean it. When the College Republicans sought to have Yiannopoulos return to campus, their request was denied on the grounds that the school couldn't provide adequate security for Yiannopoulos's "inflammatory speech."

At least one school avoided a violent suppression of speech by simply refusing Yiannopoulos a platform in the first place. New York University canceled a Yiannopoulos event, claiming there were safety concerns because the proposed venue for the speech would have been physically close to the school's Islamic Center and LGBTQ Student Center. Somehow, Yiannopoulos and his supporters were a threat to NYU's gay community, even though Yiannopoulos is himself a gay man and has never used his speeches to promote violence.

Yiannopoulos is particularly loathed by the campus left, but he's hardly the only speaker who's been silenced. When author Ann Coulter tried to give a speech at Berkeley a few weeks after Yiannopoulos, university administrators cancelled her appearance on the grounds they couldn't provide sufficient security to protect her from protesters. And then they blamed her for it.

"This is a university, not a battlefield," chancellor Nicholas Dirks declared, as if Coulter's insistence on speaking out loud was responsible for the rioting. The *New York Times* agreed, claiming without evidence that UC Berkeley had "become a target for small, militant and shadowy right-wing groups."

Across the country, students pushed to muzzle speakers they disagreed with, as administrators, politicians, and other establishment figures cheered them on. In 2014, former secretary of state Condoleezza Rice, a decidedly moderate Republican, canceled a planned speech at Rutgers University due to pressure from campus activists. The same happened to Henry Kissinger at the University of Texas, and to former Democratic senator Jim Webb at the U.S. Naval Academy, his alma mater. Brown University students forced the cancellation of a speech by former New York City Police Department commissioner Ray Kelly simply because he supported the policy of stop-and-frisk. Any deviation from orthodoxy was considered grounds for silencing.

At Middlebury College in Vermont, hundreds of angry students shut down an appearance by social scientist Charles Murray, screaming at him until he gave up trying to speak. As Murray fled the scene, protesters assaulted the faculty member escorting him, putting her in the hospital with a concussion.

The justification for attacks like this, ironically, was that certain ideas are so dangerous, they constitute violence and must therefore be squelched by force. Punching a speaker you disagree with isn't assault; it's self-defense. To many student activists, sticks and stones may break bones, but words can be lethal, and require a violent first strike.

An essay in the *Crimson*, Harvard's student newspaper, succinctly summed up the new orthodoxy: The "dedication to complete freedom of speech, regardless of whether or not the speech is harassment, [is] alarming and indicative of a larger, troubling trend in American society."

The First Amendment is "alarming"? Political differences are a crime? Students are growing up to believe that there is no longer such a thing as legitimate political debate. Free speech is a meaningless concept in a world with only one permissible set of political views; if the battle is between Good and Evil, only a fool would give Evil equal time. No wonder students at DePaul called for "hate crime" charges against classmates who used sidewalk chalk to express support for Donald Trump.

This backlash against free expression is hardly limited to public speakers. People's private remarks are being increasingly policed as well. At the University of Texas at San Antonio, a public school, philosophy grad student Alfred MacDonald was summoned to his department chair's office over remarks he had made to a fellow student. The student mentioned that she was engaged to a Muslim man. MacDonald, who is bisexual, had replied by saying he had a low opinion of Islam, since in ten Muslim-majority countries, his sexual orientation could get him put to death.

For the offense of honestly stating his views, MacDonald was threatened with punishment by department head Eve Browning.

"We have not designed our program to tolerate these behaviors," Browning said, according to a secret recording made by MacDonald. "We're not going to let you damage the program."

When MacDonald refused to apologize for expressing his opinion, Browning threatened to send him before something called the Behavior Intervention Team, and warned he could be expelled. Instead, MacDonald transferred to a new school. All that simply because MacDonald said something completely true: in many Islamic countries, his lifestyle would get him executed. But that didn't matter. MacDonald violated the sacred creed of multiculturalism. Free speech didn't stand a chance.

MacDonald's experience will grow more and more common as millennials age and take positions of leadership. A large and growing proportion of Americans under thirty, the country's most liberal cohort, don't believe in unfettered free speech. According to a Pew survey, 40 percent of millennials think the government should have the power to ban statements offensive to minority groups. A 2017 Cato Institute survey found that 52 percent of self-identified Democrats, of all ages, viewed government suppression of offensive speech as more important than the unfettered right to say whatever one wants.

A growing percentage of the country endorses not only restrictions on the First Amendment, but also the use of extralegal violence in the face of offensive ideas. In the hours after Donald Trump's inauguration in January 2017, white supremacist leader Richard Spencer was punched in the face by a stranger without provocation. The incident sparked a wave of debate, from the *New York Times* to Twitter, about whether it was okay to "punch a Nazi." One survey found that the majority of people who described themselves as "strong liberals" approved.

There isn't much scholarly disagreement about what the text of the First Amendment says about free expression. The words are unambiguous: "Congress shall make no law . . . abridging the freedom of speech, or of the press; or the right of the people peaceably to assemble." The debate is over what the term "speech" means.

In the 1980s, a group of law professors invented an extra-constitutional category known as "hate speech," which they said fell outside the protections of the First Amendment. It's not clear how they arrived at this. The Constitution says nothing about hate speech. The Supreme Court has never ruled on it. Yet on many campuses, hate speech was treated as a valid legal term with a precise and objective meaning. Symposia were held on it. Professors taught sober-sounding classes on it. Students for the most part accepted the existence of hate speech uncritically.

So did the rest of the establishment. In 2017, Howard Dean, who was not only governor of Vermont but at one point even a presidential front-runner, announced on Twitter, "Hate Speech is not protected by the First Amendment." Dean is not known for his intellectual powers, so it's possible he believed this.

—

But what accounts for CNN anchor Chris Cuomo, who is a lawyer, making an identical claim? Cuomo was once the chief law and justice correspondent for ABC News. During the debate over Milo Yiannopoulos at Berkeley, he tweeted this: "hate speech is excluded from protection. Don't just say you love the constitution . . . read it."

By the time Trump was elected, even the ACLU had given up on unfettered speech. After the group defended the right of conservative activists to rally in Charlottesville, Virginia, during the summer of 2017, some of its own staffers revolted. More than two hundred ACLU employees signed a letter complaining that the group's "broader mission" was being undermined by a "rigid stance" on free speech. The national ACLU caved, ending almost one hundred years of First Amendment absolutism.

When you sincerely believe you possess the truth, all disagreement looks like apostasy. For the greater good, it must be silenced. It's distressing when academics take this view. It's terrifying when prosecutors do.

In 2015, a Wisconsin district attorney named John Chisholm

launched an investigation into conservative activists who helped Governor Scott Walker win election. Though no actual crime had been committed, Chisholm was clearly offended that anyone would aid the Walker campaign. He and a prosecutor named Francis Schmitz ordered police to raid activists' homes, denied them access to counsel, and imposed orders that prevented them from telling anyone about what was going on. One target described the terror she felt during a predawn police raid as cops flooded into her house and seized her family's computers and cell phones. She never learned what crime she was alleged to have committed.

Wisconsin's Supreme Court ultimately intervened. The justices concluded that prosecutors had "disregarded the vital principle that in our nation and our state political speech is a fundamental right." Chisholm's contempt for the First Amendment, the court said, "assure[d] that such political speech will be investigated with paramilitary-style home invasions conducted in the pre-dawn hours and then prosecuted and punished."

The court particularly excoriated Chisholm for simply inventing new legal doctrines to suit his predetermined political purposes.

"It is utterly clear that the prosecutor has employed theories of law that do not exist in order to investigate citizens who were wholly innocent of any wrongdoing," the decision said.

In California, the state's attorney general, Xavier Becerra, filed a complaint against the Center for Medical Progress, a group of anti-abortion activists, accusing them of illegally recording their conversations with clinic operators without consent. For this, Becerra charged the organization with fifteen felonies, a response so disproportionate that even the *Los Angeles Times* couldn't find precedent for it. Tellingly, Becerra did not charge NBC for secretly recording Donald Trump on what became the now-famous *Access Hollywood* tape.

In 2015, Senator Sheldon Whitehouse announced he had uncovered a "massive and sophisticated campaign" designed to mislead Americans about climate change. Rather than rebut the "misinformation" with his own views, Whitehouse called for prosecution. Whitehouse demanded that oil companies, and their trade associations, face a federal suit under the Racketeer Influenced and Corrupt Organizations Act (RICO), the same law used to take down the mob. In Whitehouse's view, disagreement with him on climate change wasn't grounds for debate, but for prosecution.

Whitehouse wasn't alone. In 2016, Attorney General Loretta Lynch told Congress that the possibility of suing "climate deniers" had "been discussed" within the Justice Department. The department weighed the idea seriously enough to ask the FBI if a RICO case could be made.

At the state level, seventeen attorneys general teamed up to pursue similar prosecutions of heretics. California's Kamala Harris, now the state's junior U.S. senator, launched an investigation into ExxonMobil for taking a position contrary to her own on climate change. Hillary Clinton, Bernie Sanders, and Al Gore all endorsed it.

The prosecutions weren't happening fast enough for one California state senator, who introduced SB-1161, the "California Climate Science Truth and Accountability Act of 2016." The bill would have made it illegal for citizens to disseminate "scientifically inaccurate or misleading information" about climate change. Considering that scientific accuracy is always a moving target, especially on a topic as complex as climate, this amounts to the criminalization of differences of opinion.

But nowhere is speech more threatened than in Silicon Valley. In the spring of 2014, Brendan Eich became CEO of Mozilla Firefox, a company he helped found. Ten days later, he was forced to resign. Bloggers had discovered that six years earlier, Eich had donated money to Proposition 8, a referendum that banned gay marriage in California.

Proposition 8 had passed by a wide margin. Fully 70 percent of California's black population supported it. The year it became law, both Hillary Clinton and Barack Obama publicly opposed gay marriage. In 2008, Eich's position was hardly a fringe view.

None of that mattered. Eich was pushed out of his company for violating a never-specified but universally understood set of rules about what people are allowed to believe in Silicon Valley. The company marked Eich's departure with a press release celebrating Mozilla's culture of "diversity and inclusiveness." In a flourish that even by tech-company standards lacked self-awareness, Mozilla went on to boast that its "culture of openness extends to encouraging staff and community to share their beliefs and opinions in public."

In 2016, investor Peter Thiel was one of the rare Silicon Valley executives willing to donate to Donald Trump's presidential campaign. Fellow tech investors immediately demanded that Thiel lose his seat on the board of Facebook, on the grounds that supporting Trump was tantamount to committing violence. "Giving more power to someone whose ascension and behavior strike fear into so many people is unacceptable," explained Ellen Pao, herself the former head of the popular discussion site Reddit. Trump's views, Pao wrote, "are more than just political speech; fueled by hate and encouraging violence, they make each of us feel unsafe."

If tech executives will say things like this in public, it's fair to wonder how their political views affect the products they sell. It's worth worrying about. Fewer than half a dozen technology companies have an effective monopoly on the bulk of information Americans consume. What if Silicon Valley decided to let only one side speak?

The social media giant Twitter barely hides its contempt for free speech, regularly banning or locking the accounts of users for "hateful conduct," a term it keeps usefully subjective. Milo Yiannopoulos was banned by Twitter in the summer of 2016. Within a week of Donald Trump's election victory, the site carried out a purge of accounts associated with the "alt right," even if they had broken no rules. Political operative and Donald Trump adviser Roger Stone was suspended in fall 2017 for criticizing CNN personalities. Twitter awarded a verification, the blue check that signifies an account is legitimate, to the Muslim Brotherhood before it gave one to the conservative site Breitbart.

No tech company clamped down on speech more aggressively than Google, the most powerful of all. In August 2017, a Google software engineer named James Damore wrote a memo assessing the company's political culture. It could have described any large Silicon Valley company.

"At Google," wrote Damore, "we talk so much about unconscious bias as it applies to race and gender, but we rarely discuss our moral biases. Political orientation is actually a result of deep moral preferences and thus biases. Considering that the overwhelming majority of the social sciences, media, and Google lean left, we should critically examine these prejudices."

Over ten pages, Damore examined those prejudices in some detail. Notable among them is the belief that bigotry is the main impediment to professional advancement. There are fewer female engineers than male engineers, liberals believe, because men are biased against women. Damore suspected that wasn't the whole story.

"We need to stop assuming that gender gaps imply sexism," he wrote. "On average, men and women biologically differ in many ways. These differences aren't just socially constructed."

Damore, a former childhood chess prodigy with a graduate degree in biology from Harvard, was precise and nonpolemical in his assertions. In parts, he seemed nearly apologetic. "I'm simply stating that the distribution of preferences and abilities of men and women differ in part due to biological causes," he wrote, "and that these differences may explain why we don't see equal representation of women in tech and leadership. Many of these differences are small and there's significant overlap between men and women, so you can't say anything about an individual given these population level distributions."

Damore wrote the memo on a flight to China, as a way of organizing his thoughts. He never intended it to be shared beyond a circle of friends. Within a short time, the paper leaked to a popular tech blog. A political explosion followed.

Danielle Brown, Google's vice president of diversity, released a statement charging Damore with having "incorrect assumptions about gender." Brown didn't explain what those assumptions were, or how they were incorrect. She didn't need to. Nobody in the press asked. Google's CEO flew home from vacation in Europe to respond to the crisis.

Many of Damore's fellow employees, meanwhile, howled for

his dismissal. Former Google executive Yonatan Zunger wrote an op-ed saying Damore should be "escorted from the building by security and told that your personal items will be mailed to you." Others fantasized on social media about assaulting Damore.

Nearly all news organizations described the essay as an "anti-diversity memo," when in fact Damore had argued strenuously that Google's culture needed more diversity. *Vox* called it a "sexist screed," as though Damore's essay were a deranged rant and not a carefully reasoned piece.

Within days, Damore had been fired by the company. In perhaps the most Orwellian statement written since Orwell himself finished *1984*, Google explained the decision this way: "Part of building an open, inclusive environment means fostering a culture in which those with alternative views, including different political views, feel safe sharing their opinions."

In order to foster a culture in which those with alternative political views could feel safe sharing their opinions, Google fired James Damore. For the crime of sharing his alternative views. At no point did the company rebut any of the points Damore made. The fact that he made them was enough. Damore was a thought criminal, and his crime was raising the wrong questions.

The establishment applauded. Many pointed out that the First Amendment didn't apply to Damore, because Google isn't a government entity. This is a murkier area than it appears.

Government regulates all sorts of speech in the private sector. Employers can't fire workers for expressing their religious views, for example. In some states, such as California and New York, that protection extends to political beliefs. Whether Damore's firing was constitutional awaits clarification from the courts.

But what happened to James Damore is more than a legal

matter. It raises the most basic civic question of all: what kind of society do we want to live in?

Among intellectuals, the answer used to be obvious and widely agreed upon: the goal is a free society. You knew what that meant because all free societies share the same features: They tolerate dissent. They prize reason and encourage civility. They discourage witch hunts and groupthink. They try to ensure that people aren't punished for saying what they think. They recognize that truth is always a defense.

Every nation tries to influence how its citizens behave, but a free society never presumes to control what people believe. That's for the individual alone to decide.

For a moment in time, the taste-making class in America claimed to believe all of this, and the country was a better place for it. The majority of journalists and intellectuals in 1975 would never have accepted the lame excuse that silencing, firing, and ruining people for holding an opinion was fine, as long as it wasn't specifically the government doing it. They would have declared that a free country depends above all on free minds. An open society needs open discourse or else it is merely an echo chamber. They would have spoken, rallied, and sued on behalf of James Damore, Brendan Eich, and Milo Yiannopoulos.

But now, members of the same class run Google, UC Berkeley, and virtually every other powerful institution in America. Suddenly free speech looks a lot more like a threat than a virtue.

If you're wondering why prominent media figures no longer seem curious about what government agencies might be doing to Americans without their knowledge, this is the answer. For generations, journalists believed their job was to hold the powerful accountable. This very much included unelected bureaucrats committing unseen sins in the hidden recesses of the federal government. In 1975, the media raised to prominence an obscure U.S. senator from Idaho named Frank Church, after he led investigations into the activities of the CIA, NSA, FBI, and other mystery-shrouded government agencies. Church suspected the government was up to something shady. He was right.

The CIA, it turned out, had engaged in multiple assassination plots against foreign leaders, all without congressional approval or oversight. The FBI, meanwhile, seemed to have virtually every prominent person in America under surveillance, sometimes for purely political reasons. The bureau bugged Martin Luther King's hotel rooms, discovered he was an enthusiastic adulterer, and then tried to blackmail him with the information. At one point, agents sent King an unsigned letter suggesting he commit suicide.

Federal agencies opened private mail without a warrant and secretly inspected the contents. The NSA read hundreds of thousands of telegrams sent into and out of the United States. Under the pretext of fighting the Cold War, federal bureaucrats spied extensively on their fellow citizens, mostly because they could.

Reporters were outraged. Church's hearings forced a series of much-needed reforms, including the creation of congressional committees to oversee the intelligence agencies, and the passage of the Foreign Intelligence Surveillance Act to regulate domestic spying. These were heralded as meaningful achievements, bulwarks against the abuse of government power.

The Church hearings are all but forgotten today, along with the attitudes that animated them. Democrats now compete with Republicans to see who can express more admiration for law enforcement and intelligence agencies. They are joined in that by mainstream journalists.

Television news anchors spent the first months of the Trump administration sneering at the idea that government agencies might have spied on Trump advisors during the presidential campaign. Anyone who suggested it actually happened was dismissed as unstable, or a hack.

When it emerged that the Obama Justice Department had indeed spied on the Trump campaign, the posture of most in the press didn't change. CNN legal correspondent Jeff Toobin dismissed questions about the spying as "lunatic conspiracy theories." Jill Abramson, the former top editor at the *New York Times*, suggested that criticism of the Justice Department was near treasonous. "Trump's attack on the FBI is an attack on the US constitution itself," she wrote.

Meanwhile, the TV networks larded their evening lineups with retired government officials eager to defend their agencies, not to mention themselves. MSNBC hired former CIA director John Brennan as a contributor. Brennan was on the air frequently, but anchors refrained from asking about his role in the agency's targeted killing of Americans, or in the cover-up of the CIA's torture program.

Not to be outdone, CNN hired retired director of national intelligence James Clapper. Clapper was most famous for lying in testimony to Congress in 2013. "Does the NSA collect any type of data at all on millions or hundreds of millions of Americans?" Senator Ron Wyden asked. "No," Clapper replied. "Not wittingly."

A few months later, Edward Snowden leaked internal NSA documents that showed the government had scooped up the phone records of more than 100 million Americans without their knowledge or consent. Clapper had lied. Yet he was almost never asked about this on CNN. Instead Clapper was allowed to use his remaining moral authority to bat down further questions about government spying.

Journalists had become handmaidens to power. Most of them despised Donald Trump and his party. A survey during the Obama administration found not a single Republican in the White House press corps. But the main reason the press lost interest in holding the permanent government accountable is that they had more in common with its members than with the rest of the country. They share the same life experiences and cultural assumptions as the people they cover.

The people in power are the neighbors and former classmates of the members of the press. On the most basic level the two groups have become indistinguishable.

FIVE

The Diversity Diversion

What would happen if large numbers of Americans actually understood the federal tax code? All sorts of questions might arise.

Why do we tax capital at half the rate of labor? That might be the first one.

Why is it fair that some inherited-money loser living off the interest from an investment portfolio he didn't create pays half the taxes per dollar that you do? You get up every morning to go to work. He stays home, smokes weed, and watches online porn. You get hit twice as hard on April 15. He's being rewarded, while you're being punished. Is he twice as necessary as you are? Does he contribute twice as much to America?

Maybe he does. Maybe the people who wrote the tax code could explain precisely how. Maybe not. Either way, you can see how a conversation like that might quickly spin out of control and become a threat to the existing order. Better not to have it in the first place. Better to change the subject away from economics entirely.

Identity politics is a handy way to do that. It's not a coincidence that since the life expectancy of working-class whites in America has declined, elite attacks on working-class whites have escalated. White men now kill themselves at about ten times the rate of black and Hispanic women. Yet white men are consistently framed as the oppressors, particularly blue-collar white men.

This happens to be the only group in America whose average wages have declined consistently over decades. Their privilege is nevertheless a threat to the rest of us, we're told. They've managed to destroy entire cities very few of them have ever been to, from Detroit to Newark to Baltimore. They lower test scores in schools they don't attend. They cause poor nutrition, asthma, and broken families in black neighborhoods, and in their spare time exacerbate global warming. They may be dying off before their time, but working-class white men are immensely powerful.

Who came up with this story line? It's hard to know for sure, but you'd have to guess it was someone trying to cover his tracks. If you'd failed in your responsibility to the people you were in change of helping, if they started dying younger or found their drinking water contaminated with lead, you'd be very concerned about being blamed for that. You'd want people to blame one another instead. The quickest way to control a population is to turn it against itself. Divide and conquer. That's how the British ruled India.

If you wanted to run a country for the benefit of the people who lived there, by contrast, you'd do the opposite of this. You'd deemphasize racial differences. You'd understand that in a society composed of many different ethnic groups, tribalism is the greatest threat to unity and order. Of course there will always be racism, because that's the nature of people, and you'd work to discourage it. But you would resist using the existence of racism as an excuse for your failures. You would never, for example, blame an entire racial group for the sins of its ancestors. That would serve only to embitter and divide the population. It might make your job easier in the short term. But over time it would wreck your country. The ruling class once understood this.

In May 2017, Harvard University held its first ever segregated graduation ceremony. Black students have attended Harvard since just after the Civil War, and for almost 150 years they graduated alongside their white classmates, a fact the school was proud of. But in 2017, the school discarded that tradition and created something called Black Commencement, held two days before the regular graduation ceremony. Hundreds attended. Spoken-word performers reminded the audience, "we don't need the white men nor white girl pity."

Press coverage was adulatory. Boston's local NPR affiliate described the event as an opportunity for black students "to celebrate their triumphs and remember the obstacles they have faced." The *Boston Globe* agreed. "Unlike the clichéd send-offs often delivered at commencements," the newspaper explained, "the speeches at this event spoke to the political and social concerns that students of color face at an elite institution."

It's hard to overstate how strange it is to see establishment figures celebrating a black-only graduation ceremony. For generations, school integration was the one issue that united every right-thinking person in America. The educated class fought segregation everywhere they found it. They celebrated when the *Brown v. Board of Education* decision abolished "separate but equal" schools nationwide. They supported James Meredith when he integrated the University of Mississippi. They despised George Wallace and other political leaders who fought to keep black and white students apart.

They weren't satisfied with schools, either. Idealistic young members of the ruling class led the integration of restaurants, hotels, theaters, and public transportation. They argued that all human beings were equal in dignity and rights. Everyone deserved to be treated equally in the eyes of the law.

They were right about all of this. Racial segregation was wrong, and not just because black schools tended to get less state funding. Segregation divided people on the basis of things they couldn't control. It suggested that a person's race, an entirely immutable characteristic, was the most important thing about him, and should determine how he was treated by others. Segregation was dehumanizing. It reduced the individual to a faceless member of a group.

It was also, its critics often pointed out, absurd. Beneath the skin, we're all the same. Civic leaders said that constantly in the 1970s and '80s. They recited Martin Luther King speeches to drive home the point.

For decades, racial integration was the central project of American elites. Some may believe it still is. But a remarkable transformation has taken place: Elites no longer oppose segregation. They no longer insist on treating all races equally. Many instead call for segregation. They consider race the center of human identity. They demand that individuals be exalted or punished because of their skin color.

In the spring of 2018, CNN interrupted its ongoing coverage of the Russian plot to undermine democracy with a breaking story. According to several sources, Trump's interior secretary, Ryan Zinke, may have once endorsed the principle of meritocratic hiring. Zinke, a former Navy SEAL, apparently said out loud that diversity was less important than "having the right person for the right job."

CNN made it clear that this was a scandal, if not a threat to the country. Skills-based hiring? In 2018? The network ran this ominous chyron beneath the coverage: "Zinke angers many by saying it's more important to find the best people."

Washington erupted. Zinke's spokeswoman did her best to quell the fury. She assured reporters that the rumors were false. Secretary Zinke, she said, absolutely does not hire employees on the basis of their skills or ability or experience. Instead, Zinke uses criteria like genetics and physical appearance to make the call. Ryan Zinke believes in diversity.

Journalists remained skeptical. "Zinke has said he cares about excellence, and what's important is having the right person for the right job," CNN reminded viewers. "Statements like this reinforce the dated and bigoted thinking that diversity threatens quality." These ideas "threaten the security of the country."

Senator Bob Menendez of New Jersey, recently returned from an acquittal in his federal corruption trial, released a statement equating meritocratic hiring with racism. Zinke, Menendez said, is trying to create a "lily-white department."

If you've been following the evolution of elite views on race, this is all a little bewildering. It is precisely the opposite of what people like Bob Menendez were saying forty years ago. Meritocratic attitudes were once considered the answer to racism, not a manifestation of it. People should be judged on what they do, not on how they look or who their parents were or what their ancestors did. Our elites said they didn't believe in collective punishment or reward. They stood with the individual. That's why they opposed segregation.

In the fall of 2016, a protest broke out at the University of California, Berkeley. Protests over racial questions are common at Berkeley, and have long been. The campus was the site of some of the first student demonstrations against racial segregation in the early 1960s. But this protest was different. It was staged in favor of segregation.

Activists raised a banner that read, "Fight 4 Spaces of Color." They formed a human chain to block white students from entering the campus. "Whose University? Our University," they chanted. They demanded public spaces from which heterosexual whites could be excluded.

At the time, Berkeley already supported a number of race-centered facilities. The school funded an Equity Resource Center, the Fannie Lou Hamer Black Resource Center, the African American Student Development Center, the office of Native American Student Development, the Chicanx/Latinx Student Development, and the Asian/Pacific American Student Development space.

These facilities were designed for students of color, but they weren't officially limited to them. The protesters demanded space entirely off-limits to white people. Whites are a shrinking minority at Berkeley, at just 24 percent of undergraduates, but according to the protesters, any was too many. They demanded a segregated meeting area within the university's MLK student union. Nobody acknowledged the irony of banning people on the basis of skin color from a building named after Martin Luther King.

At the University of Michigan, students followed suit. They

called for school administrators to "create a permanent designated space on central campus for Black students and students of color to organize, and do social justice work." Activists criticized the existing "multicultural center" for not being "solely dedicated to community organizing and social justice work specifically for people of color." They wanted a black-only space, a segregated space. Similar demonstrations took place all over the country.

Once colleges accepted segregated public spaces, there was no reason not to segregate living quarters as well. The University of Colorado–Boulder now has housing exclusively for black students. So does the University of Connecticut. California State University, Los Angeles, maintains what it calls "black focused" housing. Cornell College in Iowa has a dormitory for black students, which the school describes as "a place of refuge for anyone who has felt discriminated against because of their race, sexuality, spirituality, gender, or ideas as a human being."

The University of Iowa offers a "Young, Gifted, and Black" community for students who seek to "strengthen knowledge and empowerment of Black students." Stanford has "ethnic theme dorms" reserved for Latinos, Asians, Native Americans, and black students.

Reed College, a liberal arts school in Oregon known for progressive politics, is at the forefront of segregating minority students. According to the school's website, its "Students of Color Community" offers nonwhite students a place "to heal together from systemic white supremacy, recover the parts of ourselves and our cultures that have been stolen through colonization, and dream new visions as we build vibrant, loving community together."

While the race politics at most colleges are driven by students, many school administrators have become enthusiastic supporters of segregation on campus. When a group of black students at Northwestern refused to allow two white students to sit at their lunch table, the school's president, Morton Schapiro, defended the exclusion in the pages of the *Washington Post*.

"Is this really so scandalous?" wrote Schapiro in an op-ed, apparently forgetting the bitter battles liberals once fought to integrate lunch counters. "Many groups eat together in the cafeteria, but people seem to notice only when the students are black. Athletes often eat with athletes; fraternity and sorority members with their Greek brothers and sisters; a cappella group members with fellow singers; actors with actors; marching band members with marching band members; and so on. . . . The white students, while well-meaning, didn't have the right to unilaterally decide when uncomfortable learning would take place."

In other words, there's nothing wrong with segregation. It's the natural order; all groups want it, and you can understand why. Even eating lunch with members of another race is, as Schapiro put it, "uncomfortable." And that's now okay with the American establishment.

Segregationists in the American South once made similar points. In his 1947 book, *Take Your Choice: Separation or Mongrelization*, Senator Theodore Bilbo of Mississippi noted that it is "to the credit of the black or Negro race in the United States that no right-thinking and straight-thinking Negro desires that the blood of his black race shall be contaminated or destroyed by the commingling of his blood with either the white or yellow races." Bilbo would have applauded as Morton Schapiro defended segregated lunch tables.

If *Brown v. Board* ruled that school segregation was illegal, how are any of these modern efforts to divide people by race legal? They quite possibly aren't. In 1983, the Supreme Court ruled that Bob Jones University should lose tax-exempt status because of its policy against interracial dating. The justices explained that the government had a legitimate interest in ending discriminatory practices and "eradicating racial discrimination."

Subsequent court decisions have upheld affirmative action, a practice that by definition discriminates on the basis of race, but only on the grounds that giving preference to nonwhite students furthers the goal of integration. Writing for the Court's majority in *Grutter v. Bollinger*, Justice Sandra Day O'Connor cited the "educational benefits that flow from student body diversity" and noted that "the skills needed in today's increasingly global marketplace can only be developed through exposure to widely diverse people, cultures, ideas, and viewpoints."

You could debate whether O'Connor was right about the global marketplace. You can't argue that segregating campus life along racial lines "increases exposure to widely diverse" people. It does just the opposite. There is nothing diverse about segregation.

For generations, it was an article of faith among elites that integration was the key to racial harmony. Bigotry grows from ignorance. That was the assumption. The more personal exposure you have to different groups, the more you'll come to see that everyone's basically the same. It may or may not have been wholly true, but it was less divisive than the alternative.

You no longer hear much from our leaders about the importance of racial harmony. Almost nobody claims we're really all the same beneath the skin. The emphasis is on our differences. That's the essence of the diversity agenda.

Not surprisingly, that has led to an explosion of racial hostility in American life. It was once considered the gravest possible sin to criticize someone for his skin color. It is now regarded as a sign of enlightenment. It's everywhere, especially on campuses:

In 2015, a sociology professor at the University of Memphis announced that Dylann Roof, the deranged Charleston church shooter, was just another example of "white people acting how they're conditioned to act."

In December 2016, a professor at Drexel tweeted, "All I want for Christmas is white genocide." Sarcasm? "To clarify," he wrote, "when the whites were massacred during the Haitian revolution, that was a good thing indeed."

A professor at the University of Hawaii posted antiwhite messages on Facebook, writing that she doesn't "trust white people." The next day, she explained: "Cis white het people need to lose more. Cis het white people don't know how to not be in control. They want to even control their dismantling of privilege."

A professor at the University of Pittsburgh observed that "we're all screwed because white people are in charge."

The State University of New York at Binghamton offered resident assistants training on "StopWhitePeople2k16."

"I sometimes don't want to be white either," explained Dr. Ali Michael of the University of Pennsylvania. Michael was referring to the story of Rachel Dolezal, the racial poseur forced to resign from the NAACP after it was revealed that she was pretending to be black. In a piece for the *Huffington Post*, Michael empathized with Dolezal, saying she faced her own crushing guilt about her whiteness. Michael said she finally concluded "that I couldn't have biological children because I didn't want to propagate my privilege biologically."

In May 2017, a black professor specializing in "critical race theory" at Texas A&M posted a video in which he speculated about when it's okay to kill white people.

In June 2017, soon after the politically motivated shooting of Republican congressman Steve Scalise, a sociology professor at Trinity College in Connecticut called white people "inhuman assholes" and tweeted the hashtag #LetThemFuckingDie. Outraged alumni withheld their donations. More than a dozen accepted students withdrew their applications. Yet the school didn't even seriously consider firing the professor.

At Evergreen State College in Washington State, students informed a white biology professor that he would have to leave campus along with his white colleagues, as an expression of atonement for their race. The professor refused to leave, on the grounds that people ought to be treated as individuals regardless of their color. Students threatened him with violence. He later resigned from Evergreen.

Several smallish, right-of-center news organizations picked up the Evergreen story. Most of the media ignored it. A white professor driven from his job by threats of racial violence? That didn't fit the approved story line. Instead, news organizations ran headlines like these:

> *Time:* The Revenge of the White Men
> *Huffington Post:* An Open Letter to White Men in America
>   (hint: it's not a love letter)
> *Atlantic:* This Is How We Lost to the White Man
> CNN: What Happens When the White Guys Are Back in
>   Charge?
> *New York Daily News:* How White Privilege Is Allowing

White Men Across the Country to Assault Black Men and
Beat the Rap
San Diego City Beat: God Give Me the Confidence of a Medio-
cre White Man

One progressive news site, *Salon*, started what was in effect
an antiwhite news beat. It produced headlines like "White Men
Are the Face of Terror," "White Guys Are Killing Us," and "The
Plague of Angry White Men."

Concerns about white racism reached levels of clinical hys-
teria in American media after Donald Trump was elected. In a
single year, 2017, news organizations ran stories about how the
following objects, icons, trends, or consumer products were effectively racist:

Credit scores

English grammar

Ice cream truck songs

Facial recognition technology

Car insurance

SAT test

Halloween costumes

Bitcoin

Milk

Wendy's

Disney movies

Pornography

Dr. Seuss books

Military camouflage

The antisegregation novel *To
Kill a Mockingbird*

The nuclear family

The song "Jingle Bells"

Tanning

Lucky Charms cereal

Mathematics

Pumpkin spice latte

Makeup

Lacrosse

Science

Star Wars

Shakespeare

Legalized marijuana

Being on time	Art history
Coca-Cola	Founding Fathers
White babies	McDonald's
The Oscars	The Bible
Wal-Mart	Craft beer
Background checks	

There were many more. Some of these stories may have been sophisticated parodies that made it past sleepy editors. Most were deadly serious. In order to justify coverage like this, you have to show that white men pose an imminent and existential threat to everyone else. Evidence for that is in short supply, so the press highlighted what they claimed was an epidemic of hate crimes. Many of those turned out to be hoaxes.

At SUNY Albany in 2016, three female black students claimed that a white mob had assaulted them while riding a public bus. The school held a public rally on their behalf. Hillary Clinton tweeted her support. A subsequent police investigation revealed the truth: the three girls had in fact started a fight and attacked the white students. They invented a fake hate crime to avoid being punished. It took police weeks to discover what actually happened, in part because the white students were too afraid to contact the police themselves.

Meanwhile, at the University of Louisiana in Lafayette, a Muslim woman claimed white men attacked her and ripped off her hijab. In Philadelphia, a black woman claimed that four white men had called her the n-word and "black bitch," and threatened to shoot her to celebrate Trump's victory. At the University of Minnesota, an Asian student said she was confronted by a white racist who demanded she "go back to Asia."

It is not clear that any of this actually happened. Dozens of other supposed hate crimes turned out to be manufactured as well. The rate of fake hate crimes appeared to outpace the rate of real ones. Yet all of these stories received extensive and credulous coverage before they were unmasked.

The narrative was clear: buried in the heart of every white person is a vial of deadly poison called racism. There is no remedy for this. Whites are born with hate built in. White racism is the indelible legacy of sins that white people committed generations ago.

This is collective race guilt. Emphasizing it eases the conscience of a certain sort of white elite. It's cathartic. It feels like an exercise in virtue, a small way to even the score. Powerful white elites secretly love to hear they're naughty.

That's why Ta-Nehisi Coates is their favorite intellectual.

———

Coates was born and raised in a tough part of West Baltimore known for crime and gangs. His father was a member of the Black Panther Party who had seven children by four women. The senior Coates also was the founder of Black Classic Press, a still-active publishing house focused on books aimed at black Americans.

Coates was an introverted boy who loved comic books. He failed eleventh-grade English but nevertheless was able to enroll in Howard University. He attended for five years but failed to graduate, in part because he failed classes on British and American literature.

Despite these setbacks, Coates launched a stuttering career in journalism. In the span of a few years, he was hired and fired by the *Philadelphia Weekly*, *Village Voice*, and *Time*. He made ends meet by working as a food deliveryman. In 2008 he landed a job with the *Atlantic*. His career took off.

To understand the Coates phenomenon, it's important to understand his audience. Coates's writings focus heavily on history, poverty, and crime, all from a black perspective. But his audience isn't black readers, the poor, or historians. Coates's most enthusiastic fans are affluent white professionals who live in coastal cities. Coates is the court theologian of the ruling class. That's not really his fault. Coates is just making a living. It's still embarrassing.

New York Times critic A. O. Scott called Coates's writing "essential, like water or air," suggesting the words aren't merely eloquent, but sacred. "Don't know if in U.S. commentary there is a more beautiful writer than Ta-Nehisi Coates," Rachel Maddow once enthused. A *New Yorker* profile concluded that a "Coates byline promises something different: intelligent ideas expressed beautifully, sentences that hit you like body blows." Author Jordan Michael Smith declared Coates "the single best writer on the subject of race in the United States."

Coates's breakout article was titled "This Is How We Lost to the White Man," a 2008 piece assessing Bill Cosby's effort to promote better parenting in the black community. The article displayed the two chief hallmarks of Coates's future essays: tremendous length (it was nearly seven thousand words long) and a meandering structure that never quite gets to the point.

"This Is How We Lost to the White Man" won numerous awards. Since its publication, every new Coates doorstopper has been met with escalating levels of ecstasy in Washington, New York, and Martha's Vineyard.

In 2014, Coates published what remains his most famous article, "The Case for Reparations." Over the course of more than fifteen thousand words, Coates describes America exclusively through the lens of racial grievance. Every significant fact of American history, Coates concludes, is a consequence of white racism. In Coates's telling, America was constructed with the labor of enslaved Africans. Racism was the basis of the country's economy, and the driving force behind its political history. The New Deal, Coates writes, "rested on the foundation of Jim Crow." The postwar housing boom was rooted in racist "redlining" policies. Decades later those policies are still the primary reason for wealth disparities in America. In a Coates essay, everything is about white racism.

Racism is omnipresent, Coates argues, and it is getting worse. To prove it, Coates cites a remark Barack Obama once made but probably didn't mean, that his daughters shouldn't benefit from affirmative action. To Coates, this is proof that racism was alive and well.

The solution is reparations. Despite the length of the essay, Coates never describes a mechanism for redistributing tax dollars to the descendants of slaves. Nor does he describe how much it might cost. He suggests the amount might be infinite.

"We may find that the country can never fully repay African Americans," Coates concludes. "Perhaps no number can fully capture the multi-century plunder of black people in America. Perhaps the number is so large that it can't be imagined, let alone calculated and dispensed."

This vagueness is frustrating, but it might be the only genuinely brilliant part of the essay. Coates knows there will never be monetary reparations for slavery. He doesn't want or need them. If he did, he'd work up a number. What he wants is a moral victory.

This desire dovetails with what his overwhelmingly white readership wants. Elites feel like good people when they read Ta-Nehisi Coates. It's exactly the kind of book you'd like to be seen bringing to the beach. What they don't want is to change their lives in any meaningful way. Coates doesn't ask them to. Admit you're bad, Coates says. Gladly, they reply. Nothing changes except how elites feel about themselves. Coates is their confessor. His books are their penance.

Coates's piece on reparations set a single-day traffic record on the *Atlantic*'s website; the paper copy sold out at many stores. The praise from organs of elite opinion was virtually unanimous. The *Washington Post* described Coates's writing as "unstinting, yet lyrical." The *New Yorker* called the essay "breathtaking." Damon Linker at the *Week* called it "the most compelling and exhaustive case for reparations that I have ever encountered," marked by Coates's "potent mixture of intelligence and passion." Carlos Lozada at the *Washington Post* described the piece as a "work of deep reporting and seething understatement [that] made Coates a literary star." FiveThirtyEight's Christie Aschwanden called it "mind-blowing." The *Baltimore Sun*'s news section called it a "ground-breaking and exhaustively researched essay." The *Huffington Post*'s Tom McKenna called it "the finest, most thorough piece of journalism I've seen in years."

After the praise came the honors. Coates won a Polk Award. He was invited to lecture at the American Library in Paris, where he was given a fellowship and asked to lecture on the history of comic books. He was named to *Politico*'s list of the fifty most impressive people in the world. His essay, *Politico* said, "stands as a powerful example of how a single author can refuse to let an issue disappear." Coates was later invited to speak about reparations at the University of Michigan, University of Chicago, University of Pennsylvania, Yale University, American University, Roosevelt University, and Grinnell.

But the peak was still to come. In 2015, Coates released his memoir, *Between the World and Me*. While Coates's articles tended to drag, the book was notably short. At thirty-seven thousand words, it could be consumed in a few hours. The book read like an extended meandering essay. It's possible his editors were too awestruck or terrified to say anything about it.

The book is a mix of autobiography and reflections on the pain of being a "black body" in America. The narrative form is a letter from Coates to his son, a concept borrowed from essayist James Baldwin's *The Fire Next Time*. It doesn't go well, partly because Coates is a leaden writer. But the main problem is that he doesn't have a lot to write about. The book is intended as a searing take on white racism in America. But the truth as it emerges over thirty-seven thousand words is that Coates doesn't seem to have experienced much racism.

Coates highlights two incidents in his life that he believes crystallize the distorting effects of white bigotry. In the first, a friend of his from college is shot and killed by a police officer. Coates opens the story this way:

> I picked up *The Washington Post* and saw that the PG County police had killed again. I could not help but think that this could have been me, and holding you—a month old by then—I knew that such loss would not be mine alone. [. . .] Then on the third day a photo appeared with

the story, and I glimpsed at and then focused on the portrait, and I saw him there. [. . .] His face was lean, brown, and beautiful, and across that face, I saw the open, easy smile of Prince Carmen Jones.

The shooting of his friend provokes several pages of reflection about how "people who believe they are white" have erected power structures dedicated to the oppression and destruction of "black bodies." Then, after six pages, Coates drops a stunner: the cop who killed his friend wasn't white. He didn't even believe he was white. He was black.

"Here is what I knew at the outset: The officer who killed Prince Jones was black," Coates writes. So how is his death evidence of white racism? Coates doesn't say.

Coates later reveals that he didn't know his slain friend particularly well. They weren't actually friends. Yet the killing of an acquaintance by a black cop made Coates feel so oppressed by white racism that when the twin towers fell on 9/11, he immediately framed the tragedy in racial terms:

I could see no difference between the officer who killed Prince Jones and the police who died, or the firefighters who died. They were not human to me. Black, white, or whatever, they were the menaces of nature; they were the fire, the comet, the storm, which could—with no justification—shatter my body.

By this point in the book, you begin to wonder if there's something psychologically wrong with Coates. A few pages later, he confirms it by describing his second life-changing brush with white racism: somebody was once rude to his son on an escalator. In his words:

> A white woman pushed you and said, "Come on!" Many things now happened at once. [. . .] There was my sense that this woman was pulling rank. I knew, for instance, that she would not have pushed a black child out on my part of Flatbush, because she would be afraid there and would sense, if not know, that there would be a penalty for such an action.

Coates understands at once that this moment is not really about an unpleasant exchange he once had with a white woman on an escalator. It's about the rotten core of America itself. It's about the degradation of black bodies: "The plunder of black life was drilled into this country in its infancy and reinforced across its history, so that plunder has become an heirloom, an intelligence, a sentience, a default setting to which, likely to the end of our days, we must invariably return."

This is nutty. It's also dumb. But more than anything, it's hostile. Coates despises white people. He doesn't hide it.

Throughout the book, he describes whiteness as a pathology. As a group, he says whites are united only by the desire to "plunder" African Americans.

> "White America" is a syndicate arrayed to protect its exclusive power to dominate and control our bodies. The power of domination and exclusion is central to the belief in being white, and without it, "white people" would cease to exist for want of reasons.

At one point in the memoir, Coates seems to get so carried away in anger that he loses control and suggests that whites are subhuman cannibals who commit atrocities simply by existing:

> There is no them without you, and without the right to break you they must necessarily fall from the mountain, lose their divinity, and tumble out of the Dream. And then they would have to determine how to build their suburbs on something other than human bones, how to angle their jails toward something other than a human stockyard, how to erect a democracy independent of cannibalism. I would like to tell you that such a day approaches when the people who believe themselves to be white renounce this demon religion and begin to think of themselves as human. But I can see no real promise of such a day. We are captured, brother, surrounded by the majoritarian bandits of America.

It goes on like this. In the final two paragraphs, the book takes an abrupt turn and blames white people for environmental degradation and global warming. Whites, whom Coates has decided to call "Dreamers," have destroyed not simply races of people, but the natural landscape itself. Wrecking things is what they do. As Coates puts it:

> The Dreamers have improved themselves, and the damming of seas for voltage, the extraction of coal, the transmuting of oil into food, have enabled an expansion in plunder with no known precedent. And this revolution has freed the Dreamers to plunder not just the bodies of humans but the body of Earth itself.

163

Between the World and Me is an unusually bad book: poorly written, intellectually flabby, relentlessly shallow and bigoted. No honest reader with an IQ over 100 could be impressed by it. One presumes that the moment America wakes up from its current fever, Coates's memoir will be forgotten immediately, an embarrassing relic from an embarrassing time.

It's a measure how thoroughly the diversity cult has corroded the aesthetic standards of our elites that the book was greeted with almost unanimous praise, which is to say, lying. *Publishers Weekly* described it as "compelling, indeed stunning . . . rare in its power to make you want to slow down and read every word. This is a book that will be hailed as a classic of our time."

Between the World and Me won the National Book Award, as well as the NAACP Image Award. It was a finalist for the Pulitzer Prize and National Book Critics Circle Award. It was listed as among the finest books of 2015 by the *New York Times Book Review*, *O: The Oprah Magazine*, *Washington Post*, *People*, *Entertainment Weekly*, *Vogue*, *Los Angeles Times*, *San Francisco Chronicle*, *Chicago Tribune*, *New York*, *Newsday*, and *Publishers Weekly*. It was a number-one *New York Times* bestseller.

In the fall of 2015, Coates was given a $625,000 MacArthur Fellowship, not that he needed the money by that point. In early 2018, Harlem's iconic Apollo Theater adapted his book into a multimedia performance, with excerpted monologues and pro-jected video, all set to a score by jazz pianist Jason Moran.

One of the book's many fans was black separatist Gavin Long. In 2016, Long assassinated three police officers in Baton Rouge, Louisiana. On his personal "MAN-datory Reading List," Long listed *Between the World and Me* at number two. It was a rare second-place finish for Ta-Nehisi Coates.

Between the World and Me remains Coates's most famous work, but his star has hardly dimmed since then. His every literary endeavor is now national news. In 2016, Coates became the writer for the Marvel comic book *Black Panther*, about a black superhero.

In 2018, he began writing a Captain America series as well.

When not writing comic books, Coates has continued to write magazine articles. Following Donald Trump's 2016 victory, he wrote an essay titled "The First White President," attributing Trump's victory, not surprisingly, to white supremacy.

"Trump, more than any other politician, understood the valence of the bloody heirloom and the great power in not being a nigger," Coates writes in the piece. Coates restates this point, his only point, repeatedly and floridly: "To Trump, whiteness is neither notional nor symbolic but is the very core of his power. In this, Trump is not singular. But whereas his forebears carried whiteness like an ancestral talisman, Trump cracked the glowing amulet open, releasing its eldritch energies."

And so, having shattered a supernatural amulet, the first white president was born.

"Certainly not every Trump voter is a white supremacist, just as not every white person in the Jim Crow South was a white supremacist," Coates concedes, generously. "But every Trump voter felt it acceptable to hand the fate of the country over to one."

In fact, Trump outperformed Mitt Romney with black and Hispanic voters. Coates does not address this. His enthralled white readers didn't ask him to. Coates told them exactly what they wanted to hear. They were grateful for that.

It's revealing that the one group of reviewers persistently

resistant to Coates's brilliance is black intellectuals. In general, they haven't been impressed by his books.

They feel no need to be.

—

Jason Hill, a DePaul University philosophy professor, published an open-letter response to *Between the World and Me*. The book, Hill concluded, "reads primarily like an American horror story and, I'm sorry to say, a declaration of war against my adopted country."

Hill, a gay Jamaican immigrant who came to the United States as an adult, says he found a very different country than the one Coates describes. In America, he writes, he could escape "the blight of Jamaican homophobia" and "find peace and true love and be left alone to pursue my dream."

"Your beliefs threaten to alienate your son from his country and afflict him with a sense of moral inefficacy and impotence," Hill added. "This could squash his chance of being an engine of change in the course of history."

Yet even as an immigrant to America, Hill understood perfectly well Coates's appeal to elites: "Your accusations have made for interesting dinner talk among the cognoscenti and literati in liberal bourgeois enclaves, where some believe moral masochism and symbolic self-flagellation are signs of virtue," he wrote.

Cedric Johnson, a professor of African American studies at the University of Illinois, made a similar argument, perceiving that Coates's focus on racial conflict in fact served to entrench the powerful.

"Race-first politics are often the means for advancing discrete, bourgeois class interests," Johnson wrote for the left-wing

Jacobin magazine. "From the antebellum anti-slavery struggles to the postwar southern desegregation campaigns to contemporary battles against austerity, interracialism and popular social struggle have been central to improving the civic and material circumstances of African Americans."

Equally damning was the critique of Princeton professor Cornel West. West accused Coates of being "the neoliberal face of the black freedom struggle," responsible for "fetishizing white supremacy." Rather than engage with West's criticism, Coates quit Twitter.

Thomas Chatterton Williams, a contributing writer to the *New York Times Magazine* and a fellow at the American Academy in Berlin, was even tougher on Coates, accusing him of sharing the same assumptions of white supremacists. Both, he writes, "eagerly reduce people to abstract color categories, all the while feeding off of and legitimizing each other, while those of us searching for gray areas and common ground get devoured twice."

Maybe the hardest criticism came from Columbia University professor John McWhorter, who is black. "My issue with the Coates phenomenon is that I find it racist," McWhorter said. White critics are "letting pass as genius something they never would if it was not a black person doing it."

This is a deep point, and one wonders if Coates has considered it himself. Why would a racist nation bother to pretend *Between the World and Me* is a smart book?

Or maybe the fact that critics feverishly maintained the pretense proves Coates's point: only a racist country would so disingenuously praise a mediocre black writer. Either way, there's no question that irresponsible rhetoric like Coates's, and the equally irresponsible response it received from elites, was inflaming racial tension in America. Yelling about imaginary racism was making people hate one another.

At Berkeley in the fall of 2017, a group of students disrupted a midterm exam in a class on American labor issues. They claimed the professor was unsuited to teach the class, not because he lacked credentials, but because he was a white man. When other students asked to be allowed to take the test anyway, they were ordered to remain silent. They were too white to talk.

"White people, shut up!" one protester shouted.

"You [white people] fucking take so much space. You talk so much already," said another. Complaining about being attacked on the basis of your race was itself racist.

In July 2016, a black man assassinated five police officers and injured nine others in Dallas. The city's police chief, who was black, left no doubt about motive: "The suspect stated he wanted to kill white people, especially white officers."

Here's what Hillary Clinton tweeted the next day: "White Americans need to do a better job of listening when African Americans talk about the seen and unseen barriers you face every day."

At the funeral for the slain officers, Barack Obama took the opportunity to lecture the officers' family members about the racism of America's police departments: "We also know that centuries of racial discrimination, of slavery, and subjugation, and Jim Crow; they didn't simply vanish with the law against segregation . . . we know that bias remains," he said to children who had just lost their fathers in the attack. "No institution is entirely immune, and that includes our police departments. We know this.

"When all this takes place," Obama continued, "more than fifty years after the passage of the Civil Rights Act, we cannot simply turn away and dismiss those in peaceful protest as troublemakers or paranoid."

Listening to Obama, it was easy to forget that the killer was a black man, and that the cops he murdered had been protecting a Black Lives Matter protest.

————

When Democratic political consultants looked at the exit polling data from the 2016 election, trying to figure out what happened, many were shocked by the high number of white Democrats who'd voted for Donald Trump. Various experts tried to explain the trend. Was it sexism? Russian propaganda? Hillary's failure to campaign in the upper Midwest? Almost nobody suggested the obvious: if voters think you hate them for how they were born, they won't vote for you.

This lesson didn't penetrate. Days after Trump's inauguration, Democrats held elections for a new DNC chair. One of the candidates was Sally Boynton Brown, the executive director of the Democratic Party of Idaho. Brown said that if elected, she would make it her mission "to shut other white people down." She promised to seek advice from "people of color . . . because you have the answers." With those answers, Brown pledged to "school the other white people."

Keith Ellison isn't white, but he agrees with Brown. The Minnesota congressman was also running for DNC chair, and he has similar views on race. Ellison once proposed the formation of a black ethno-state, on land taken from the United States and funded by reparations paid by white people. At the time,

Ellison described the Constitution as the "best evidence of a white racist conspiracy to subjugate other peoples." Ellison got the endorsement of Senators Bernie Sanders, Elizabeth Warren, and Harry Reid.

Supporting people like Keith Ellison is the price the establishment pays for leaving the economic status quo untouched. If you can convince voters that white supremacy in the heartland is the real problem, it's possible they may ignore that you and your family live in a rarified white enclave and are far richer now than you were ten years ago.

This is why the loudest voices against white racism live in the whitest places. A 2014 study by researchers at the University of California, Los Angeles, found New York State's public schools the most segregated in America, and "the leader in segregating its Latinos." Remarkably, black students in New York are more likely to attend segregated schools than those who live in the South.

The division becomes more profound in New York City. Fully 73 percent of the city's charters qualify as "apartheid schools," meaning they're less than 1 percent white; 90 percent were "intensely segregated," at less than 10 percent white.

The city's schools become more segregated every year. In 1989, when the establishment still supported integration, a typical black student in New York would have attended a public school that was 21 percent white. By 2010, the mix had dropped to 17 percent white.

Why is this happening? One reason is that rich New Yorkers would rather not have their children go to school with minorities. Comedian Samantha Bee may be one of these. Bee expresses all the fashionable racial views you'd expect given her politics and income level. "It's pretty clear who ruined America," Bee once said. "White people."

Bee doesn't mean it. She lives on the Upper West Side of Manhattan, which is two-thirds white, far higher than the city's average. Her children attended a 64 percent white school with an overwhelmingly affluent student body. When, in an effort to increase diversity, city officials tried to relocate the school to across the street from a housing project, Bee and her husband objected. Diversity is fine. But moving the school would have lowered property values. Our elites may despise white people, but they want to make certain their kids go to school with them.

How did Bee and her neighbors respond to the proposed increase in diversity? With rage and defiance. "We were sad to learn that [there aren't a lot of African Americans who live on the Upper West Side]," one local parent told a reporter. "But we chose to move to this place because we put the quality of the education at a higher value." In other words, we live here because it isn't very diverse.

Something similar happened recently in the DUMBO neighborhood of Brooklyn. The city proposed moving kids from the mostly white school in the neighborhood to a mostly black school nearby. Parents opposed it.

Who are these bigots? The richest people in Brooklyn. The neighborhood supported Hillary Clinton with more than 90 percent of the vote in the 2016 election.

In nearby Park Slope, Brooklyn, which is almost as affluent as DUMBO, another forced integration drama played out in almost exactly the same way. One parent complained to the *New York Times* that she felt the city was conducting an "experiment" on her children by placing them in a heavily black school.

You may recall that working-class parents in South Boston made strikingly similar remarks in the 1970s, when a federal judge bused their children into black neighborhoods for school. They thought their kids were being subjected to reckless social experiments, too. Parents in Little Rock said the same thing when President Dwight Eisenhower sent the 101st Airborne to integrate Central High School. The establishment denounced them all as racist.

If you want to know what people really care about, take a look at where they live, especially if they could live anywhere. Hillary and Bill Clinton are worth tens of millions of dollars and have free Secret Service protection for life. They could live safely in Harlem or East New York. Instead they bought a place in Chappaqua, which is less than 2 percent black.

Barack and Michelle Obama are also rich and surrounded by bodyguards. Their kids went to Sidwell Friends, so school zoning is irrelevant to them. Yet when they left the White House they still moved to the whitest neighborhood in Washington. Fewer than 4 percent of their neighbors are black, in a town that was known for generations as Chocolate City.

Mayor Bill de Blasio of New York is a tireless advocate for diversity, but not in his own neighborhood. Although he lives in Brooklyn, where one in three residents is African American, his own zip code is one of the whitest in New York. It's less than 5 percent black.

Massachusetts senator Elizabeth Warren, meanwhile, doesn't really live on an Indian reservation. She lives in Cambridge, Massachusetts, home of Harvard, as well as an enormous number of white people. Her zip code is less than 6 percent black.

Even Representative Maxine Waters of Los Angeles, an open black nationalist, doesn't choose to live around the people she represents. Waters doesn't live within the bounds of her own district. She lives in a six-thousand-square-foot, $4.3 million spread in Hancock Park, one of the wealthiest neighborhoods in Los Angeles. How did Waters afford a house that expensive after forty years of working in government? I asked once. She didn't answer, but did call me a racist.

But what's more interesting are the demographics of the neighborhood where Waters lives. The district she represents in Congress has the second-highest percentage of African American residents in the state. The neighborhood where Waters bought her mansion is just 6 percent black—or, as she might put it if she didn't live there, it's 1950s-level segregated.

Washington, D.C., is one of America's wealthiest cities, and one of its most progressive. Fully 91 percent of the city voted for Hillary Clinton, the highest percentage of any city in America. But political homogeneity hasn't produced diverse neighborhoods. According to statistician Nate Silver at FiveThirtyEight, Washington is America's sixth-most-segregated city. The most segregated city, Chicago, gave Clinton 84 percent of its votes in 2016.

Elites choose to live in cocoons white enough to burn your retinas, even as they mock the middle of the country as the land of mayonnaise and Wonder Bread and Klan rallies. For all their professed enthusiasm for America's melting pot, they don't mix and don't want to.

Meanwhile the identity politics they espouse makes the country easier to govern, even as it makes it much harder to live in. Identity politics is based on the premise that every American is a member of a subgroup, usually a racial category. The point of achieving political power is to divert resources to your group. Another word for this is tribalism.

This is the most divisive possible way to run a country. Because they are not about ideas, and instead based on inborn characteristics, tribalism and identity politics are inherently unreasonable. There's no winning arguments, or even having them. There is only victory or defeat for the group. Your gain is my loss, by definition. It's zero-sum.

Right now, the fault line is between whites and nonwhites. But as America grows more racially diverse, rifts will inevitably open between more groups. In a tribal system, every group finds itself at war with every other group. It's the perfect perversion of the American ideal: "Out of many, one" becomes "Out of one, many." This is the unhappy, blood-soaked story of countless civilizations around the world. It never ends well.

But it does make for effective electoral politics, and that's the point. There's no faster way to mobilize voters than to stoke their racial fears, while promising to deliver for their particular tribe. It's irresistible. At the moment, the coalition of identity groups has held together because it is united in single purpose against white male power. But rapid demographic change makes this unsustainable. When the traditional scapegoat becomes insufficient, various factions will turn on one another. Chaos will ensue.

———

America got a glimpse of what this might look like within hours of Donald Trump's inauguration. Horrified by what had just happened, a group of politically minded scientists began planning a protest against the incoming administration. "Scientists have battled the political and ideological forces against concepts such as evolution and climate change for years," explained Stanford biology professor Elizabeth Hadly. "We have patiently articulated the physical and biological laws governing the universe."

Despite the patient articulation, Donald Trump didn't seem to be listening. At times the new president appeared skeptical of global warming orthodoxy. There were reports that he planned to cut funding for scientific research.

Organizers decided to respond with what they called the March for Science, a series of protests staged in more than six hundred cities on Earth Day, with the primary march in Washington, D.C. The point was to show that educated people support science, as they always have. From Galileo, to the Scopes trial, to the modern debate over climate, elites have championed the scientific method and evidence-based decision making in the face of sometimes violent opposition. City dwellers trust facts. Rural people don't. Everybody in Northwest D.C. knows this. "I believe in science!" Hillary Clinton boasted as she accepted the Democratic Party's nomination. The crowd went wild.

Excitement about the science march ran high on Facebook. The *New York Times* and *Washington Post* ran approving previews. Protesters readied their signs: "Science is not a liberal conspiracy"; "Defiance for science"; "Science is resistance." Bill Nye, a children's show host known as "the Science Guy," signed on as an honorary chair.

It looked like a promising start, but it wasn't long before the March for Science ran into trouble, all of it internal. The main problem was the leadership of the event. It was insufficiently diverse: too white, and too male. Strictly speaking, this shouldn't have been relevant; the race of researchers doesn't affect the outcome of scientific experiments, their ability to achieve scientific insight, or for that matter, their ability to advocate on behalf of science research and funding. But in the racially aware context of 2017, a purported lack of diversity was a huge problem.

After much debate, march organizers decided to establish a connection between the hard sciences, which they were ostensibly defending, and broader issues of concern to activists. "Colonization, racism, immigration, native rights, sexism, ableism, queer-, trans-, intersex-phobia and economic justice are scientific issues," organizers declared on Twitter ahead of the march.

Intersex-phobia, a scientific issue? Indeed, insisted organizers. "At the March for Science," their website read, "we are committed to centralizing, highlighting, standing in solidarity with, and acting as accomplices with black, Latinx, Asian and Pacific Islander, indigenous, non-Christian, women, people with disabilities, poor, gay, lesbian, bisexual, queer, trans, non-binary, agender, and intersex scientists and science advocates."

Even the group's diversity statement was a political battlefield; it was updated multiple times after critics complained that it didn't mention the disabled or have sufficient language promoting inclusion.

It was never clear what "centralizing" intersex Pacific Islanders had to with science. Working scientists, including nonwhite ones, were perplexed as well. Sylvester James Gates, an African American physicist who served on Barack Obama's presidential science council, was one of them. Gates worried that "such a politically charged event might send a message to the public that scientists are driven by ideology more than by evidence."

Gates had reason for concern. Organizers added "immigration bans" to the list of "scientific" issues the march planned to address. Days before the event, the group cited the Trump administration's bombing of Islamic State positions in Afghanistan as an "example of how science is weaponized against marginalized people."

In the end, the whole event was poisoned by the toxin of interest group politics. Legitimate scientists dropped out or decided not to go. As one put it, the March for Science had been "hijacked by the kind of political partisanship it should instead be concerned about."

At the same time, the organizers were criticized for not being sufficiently committed to identity politics. Jacquelyn Gill, an ecologist and University of Maine professor, quit the organizing committee over what she called a "toxic, dysfunctional environment and hostility to diversity and inclusion." No matter how quickly the march's organizers ran from legitimate science, it wasn't fast enough.

In Memphis, the march finally split along racial lines. A primarily white leadership led one demonstration, activists of color led the other. Even science couldn't withstand the pressures of identity politics.

———

There was a moment when tribalism in American politics wasn't inevitable. In the summer of 2004, Barack Obama was a candidate for the U.S. Senate from Illinois. In August he gave the keynote address at the Democratic convention in Boston. It was probably the last time a prominent Democrat will ever endorse the traditional goals of the civil rights movement before a national television audience.

"There's not a black America and white America and Latino

America and Asian America; there's the United States of America," Obama said to the cheering stadium. "We are one people, all of us pledging allegiance to the stars and stripes, all of us defending the United States of America."

Before the decade was out, race baiter Al Sharpton would be a regular in the White House. Obama invited Sharpton more than seventy times to seek his advice on domestic policy.

Nobody in Barack Obama's world even pretends there is still one America. There are now as many Americas as there are hyphenated identities. The 2016 Democratic platform includes the acronym "LGBT" nineteen times and "African" or "black" fifteen times. "Mexican," "Latino," or "Hispanic" together appear seven times, as does "transgender." The word "Muslim" appears six times, "Asian" five. "Pacific Islanders" receives six mentions, while "Native Americans" and "Indians" get thirty-eight. And so on.

Another hyphenated category, "white-Americans," made it into the Democratic platform, but only as the subject of hostility. There are four references to white people in the platform. The first describes it as "unacceptable" that whites earn more on average than African Americans and Latinos. The next points out that it's also "unacceptable" that African American arrest rates are higher than those for whites. Interestingly, Asians make more than whites, and also have lower incarceration rates, yet those stats go unmentioned.

The third reference laments the fact that African Americans and Latinos lost their jobs faster than whites during the last recession. In the fourth and final reference to whites, the platform complains that Donald Trump "plays coy" with white supremacists.

The last charge says a lot about the fantasy life of our elites.

There aren't many open white supremacists left in America. In a nation with almost 200 million white people, the various factions of the Ku Klux Klan have fewer than ten thousand members between them. Other racist groups are even smaller. None of these people have much power.

This could change, but it won't change because of Donald Trump. White identity politics will be a response to a world in which identity politics is the only game there is. In a country where virtually every nonwhite group reaps advantages from being racially conscious and politically organized, how long before someone asks the obvious question: why can't white people organize and agitate along racial lines, too?

People have asked the question before, of course, but so far they've been self-discrediting: haters, morons, and charlatans. What happens when someone calm and articulate does it?

It will be a simple argument to make. Soon whites will be a minority in America. They've got enemies, as the establishment often demonstrates, as well as interests to protect. Is there some rational reason, someone will ask, why they should be the only group in America not allowed to think of themselves as a group?

At this rate, that will happen. How could it not? When it does, when white people become another interest group fighting for the spoils, America as we've known it will be over.

The economy may continue to hum along. We'll still have elections and fire departments and stop signs, many of the trappings of the country you remember. But the sense that we're all in this together, united by citizenship in a common endeavor of some kind, as Americans? That will end forever.

We'll miss it.

SIX

Elites Invade the Bedroom

What if a small group of unhappy people got to write the rules for your personal life? Would you be concerned? Common sense suggests it's wiser to take advice from people who've had demonstrable success in the areas they're advising on. That's why there aren't a lot of homeless real estate brokers or obese personal trainers. Bankrupt investment advisors have a tough time too. Nobody wants to hire them.

If you were looking for someone to tell you how to live, you'd screen candidates based on the success of their own lives. You'd be looking for people who were happily married over a long period, with well-adjusted children who respected them. You'd want to know if they had stable, honest friendships. Sanity would be a key requirement, so you'd check that, too. A cheerfully self-deprecating sense of humor might be one sign of emotional health. Calm self-confidence might be another. If you found a person like that, you'd have a role model.

Have you ever met a professional feminist who fit that description? That's a serious question, not a dig. There are surely happy feminists out there, living on goat farms in Oregon and making organic soap. It might be worth asking them the secret to their contentment. But they're not part of the national conversation. They're not on Twitter at midnight enforcing codes of behavior on the rest of us. They're not giving dating advice to teenage girls in *Cosmopolitan* magazine. They're not running the women's studies department at your daughter's college.

The people who are might be the single unhappiest group in America. Not one of them has a personal life you'd care to emulate. You wouldn't want to have dinner with them. They're neurotic, miserable people.

Yet somehow this same group has acquired enormous power over our society. They presume to set the standards for the most intimate and elemental questions of human existence: Who has sex with whom and under what circumstances. What it means to be male or female. How to treat your spouse. How to raise children.

Many of their ideas about these things are ludicrous. Some are fail-safe recipes for tragedy. But you can't flout their rules in public without fear of being punished. How did this happen?

It all began innocently enough. In 1963, a mother of three from Rockland County, New York, wrote a book about affluent housewives like herself. Her name was Betty Friedan. She called the book *The Feminine Mystique*. It described the frustrated loneliness of women pushed young into marriage and motherhood.

"Each suburban wife struggled with it alone," Friedan wrote. "As she made the beds, shopped for groceries, matched slipcover material, ate peanut butter sandwiches with her children, chauffeured Cub Scouts and Brownies, lay beside her husband at night—she was afraid to ask even of herself the silent question—'Is this all?'"

The book sold more than three million copies, and ultimately helped define modern feminism. Friedan divorced her husband and founded the National Organization for Women. The movement Friedan inspired grew to become a defining force in American life. At times, feminists were radical and angry. Yet there was nothing militant about *The Feminine Mystique*. In retrospect its demands seem reasonable, even obvious.

"In almost every professional field, in business and in the arts and sciences, women are still treated as second-class citizens," Friedan wrote. "A girl should not expect special privileges because of her sex, but neither should she 'adjust' to prejudice and discrimination."

The book ended not with a call to arms, but a question: "Who knows what women can be when they are finally free to become themselves?"

More than fifty years later, we know the answer. In 2018, more girls than boys will graduate from high school, and with higher grades. That's not surprising, given that women's IQ scores are rising faster than men's are. Since about 1980, women have been more likely than men to go to college, as well as to stay there and graduate, and that trend has dramatically accelerated. The average four-year campus is now 55 percent female.

Women still live longer than men, as they always have, but now they have better credit ratings, too. Single women buy homes at more than twice the rate of single men. For the first time since cars replaced horses, more women than men have driver's licenses. When they run for political office, women are as likely as men to win elections.

Women now constitute the majority of professional workers in the United States. Most managers are female. The wage gap between men and women has shrunk to almost nothing. In some jobs, women already make more than men.

By the standards set forth in *The Feminine Mystique*, the women's movement succeeded. Feminism was created to open up opportunities for women, and it did. But how do the beneficiaries feel about it? Did feminism make women happy?

We don't have to speculate. Since 1972, researchers at the University of Chicago have collected data for a project called the General Social Survey. The purpose is to measure the changing attitudes of Americans. They've discovered a lot of interesting things, but maybe the most striking is this: women have become dramatically less happy over the past forty years.

In the early years of the study, women reported greater happiness than men. They've become progressively less content ever since. Men are now considerably more satisfied with their lives than women are. That's true across demographic groups, regardless of income. It's not about money.

"To put that in perspective," explained one researcher, "this decline in happiness is comparable to the effects of an eight and a half percentage point increase in unemployment." But women aren't unemployed. They work more, and earn more, than they did in 1972. It hasn't helped.

In fact, research suggests it may be part of the problem. Marriages in which the female partner earns more than her husband are more likely to report instability and ultimately end in divorce. By contrast, a study of twelve years of data from the

GSS found that women who reported having more traditional views on gender roles within the family "reported higher marital and individual happiness." Studies of attitudes in other countries (Switzerland, for example) have found roughly the same thing. And there's this:

"A study published in the journal *American Sociological Review* used longitudinal survey data from 1980 to 1988 and found that as wives' attitudes became more egalitarian their perceived marital quality declined. Interestingly, for husbands, as their attitudes became more egalitarian their perceived marital quality increased."

Findings like these challenge what we're told is true about families and gender roles. You'd think professional feminists would be eager to understand what the research means, since bringing happiness to women was supposed to be the whole point of feminism. They're not. Feminists have by and large ignored the data. Maybe they don't want to know. More likely, they just don't care.

What began as a liberation movement has narrowed to become cultish and sectarian, a strange parody of its former self. Betty Friedan argued that all women should have the widest possible range of life choices. Modern feminists demand that women meet a set of expectations every bit as confining as anything 1950s suburbia imposed.

None is more rigid than the feminist orthodoxy surrounding abortion. In January 2017, a women's group from Texas called the New Wave Feminists signed on as a sponsor of the Women's March on Washington, a massive protest staged to coincide with Trump's inauguration. The group seemed to meet all the necessary criteria for the event. They were women, they were feminists, and they were deeply offended by Donald Trump. As it happens, they were also opposed to abortion.

When organizers of the march discovered that last fact, they revoked the group's credentials. "We look forward to marching on behalf of individuals who share the view that women deserve the right to make their own reproductive decisions," they said in a statement, explaining that the credentials had been granted "in error."

Feminists applauded the exclusion. "Intersectional feminism does not include a pro-life agenda," explained writer Roxane Gay. "That's not how it works! The right to choose is a fundamental part of feminism."

It's not obvious why abortion should be the one nonnegotiable value of feminism, or even a value at all. The earliest feminists saw nothing virtuous about it. Elizabeth Cady Stanton, one of the first suffragettes, called abortion the "murder of children." Susan B. Anthony referred to it as "infanticide."

Nor did they see anything shameful about childbearing and motherhood. On the contrary, early feminists understood their power as women was rooted in their biological differences from men. Only women bear children. Having children may not be the most consequential thing an individual woman does, and not all women choose to do it. But childbearing remains women's unique contribution to the perpetuation of the species. Without pregnant women, humanity dies. That's not a small thing. Pretending it is denies biology.

But there's a larger cost. Promoting abortion diminishes the importance of childbearing. You can't simultaneously argue that pregnancy is meaningful, and that ending a pregnancy is as morally significant as an appendectomy. Both can't be true. When motherhood is less valuable to society, so are women.

Yet modern feminists behave as if fertility is a threat to be feared and conquered. They devalue the one irreplaceable thing women do. They clearly believe that having children is less impressive than working at an investment bank.

It's hard to see how any of this makes women more powerful. Indeed it sounds like an argument a man might make to undermine women. If there's going to be a war of the sexes, most men would rather have women compete on male terms, without the advantage of their unique female qualities. If you wanted to dominate women, you'd tell them to act like men.

There was a time when feminists paid lip service to the idea that there's something regrettable about abortion. Most people sense there is, so feminists included "rare," along with "safe and legal," when they described what they thought abortion should be. No longer.

"Abortion isn't a bad thing, so we shouldn't be talking about it like it is," declared a 2014 article on EverydayFeminism.com, a popular feminist website. In 2015, activists launched the Shout Your Abortion campaign, calling for abortion to be treated as an unambiguous social good. "Plenty of people still believe that on some level—if you are a good woman—abortion is a choice which should be accompanied by some level of sadness, shame, or regret," said one of the campaign's founders, Amelia Bonow. "But you know what? I have a good heart and having an abortion made me happy in a totally unqualified way."

In 2017, the *Atlantic* ran a piece by Moira Weigel attacking ultrasound technology because it was capable of convincing women not to have abortions. "These images produced a new and unprecedented vision of human development," Weigel wrote. Seeing a child in utero with that level of clarity might spoil the entire experience.

But abortion isn't always a matter of personal liberation, especially outside the affluent West. Sex-selective abortions are common in countries with a strong cultural preference for sons, like India and China. Studies show they always result in fewer daughters. If you believed your job was to defend women, you'd be bothered by that.

Feminists aren't. In 2013, Sarah Ditum wrote a piece in the *Guardian* titled "Why Women Have a Right to Sex-Selective Abortion." Ditum's reasoning: "As far as I'm concerned, it doesn't matter why any woman wants to end her pregnancy . . . even the most terrible reason for having an abortion holds more sway than the best imaginable reason for compelling a woman to carry to term."

In May 2012, Planned Parenthood, the country's largest provider of abortions, affirmed the same position. In a statement, the group declared that "no Planned Parenthood clinic will deny a woman an abortion based on her reasons for wanting one, except in those states that explicitly prohibit sex-selective abortions."

In other words, abortion is more important than girls. In 1998, Nina Burleigh, *Time* magazine's former White House correspondent, put it as succinctly as anyone ever has as she defended Bill Clinton from charges of sexual harassment. "I would be happy to give him a blowjob just to thank him for keeping abortion legal," Burleigh said. "I think American women should be lining up with their Presidential kneepads on to show their gratitude for keeping the theocracy off our backs."

Nine years later, in 2007, Burleigh remained unapologetic about her remarks. "I thought it was high time for someone to tweak the white, middle-aged beltway gang taking Clinton to task for sexual harassment," she wrote in a piece for the *Huffington Post*. "The insidious use of sexual harassment laws to bring down a president for his pro-female politics was the context in which I spoke."

This is an odd interpretation of events. Republicans did try to bring Clinton down. They impeached him, which in retrospect seems unwise and disproportionate. But in what sense was Bill Clinton "pro-female"?

Clinton received oral sex from a twenty-two-year-old intern named Monica Lewinsky. When the story became public, he and his wife attacked Lewinsky as delusional and a "stalker." The ensuing publicity destroyed Lewinsky's life. The Clintons never apologized to her, or even suggested they felt remorse.

A series of other women credibly accused Bill Clinton of sex crimes, including groping, assault, and forcible rape. All of the accusers were partisan Democrats who had once supported Clinton and his political agenda. They did not accuse him anonymously, but on camera in public, and in some cases under oath. All of them bolstered their claims with evidence, including the testimony of friends to whom they told their stories contemporaneously.

They were serious women, making serious claims. They were savaged by the Clintons and their allies as delusional opportunists. Most revealingly, they were dismissed on class grounds, as greedy proles. In the words of one of the Clintons' closest advisors, these women were the kind of people who turn up "when you drag a $100 bill through a trailer park."

For the feminists who still believed in the values of *The Feminine Mystique*, this must have been a shocking moment. In the traditional feminist catechism, there is no greater offense than

189

attacking self-described victims of sexual assault. You believe them, or at least take their claims seriously. Yet feminist groups remained silent as the White House dismissed the women as dishonest and hysterical.

How could feminists participate in this? Simple: Clinton had vetoed two partial-birth abortion bans. That was enough to indemnify him from criticism, even if it meant that innocent women were slandered. Abortion isn't something that matters to feminists. It's all that matters. It excuses anything.

In the summer of 1969, Senator Ted Kennedy went to a party on a small island adjacent to Martha's Vineyard, Massachusetts, called Chappaquiddick. A little before midnight, he left in his Oldsmobile with a young unmarried aide named Mary Jo Kopechne. Apparently drunk, Kennedy accidentally drove off the side of a narrow wooden bridge into a tidal canal. The car landed upside down, but Kennedy swam to safety. He left Mary Jo Kopechne in the car.

Kennedy fled the scene and went to bed. Likely afraid of being charged with drunk driving, he did not alert authorities.

Fishermen found Kopechne's body the next morning. Divers estimated that she had survived for several hours in the Oldsmobile, her head in an air pocket, until she finally suffocated from lack of oxygen. She could easily have been saved if Kennedy had called for help.

The scandal that followed likely ended Kennedy's presidential aspirations, but it did nothing to dim his popularity with feminists. Kennedy was an absolutist on legal abortion. That was more important than the killing of an individual woman.

When Kennedy died in 2009, feminists celebrated his life. The *Huffington Post* ran a piece asking, "What would Mary Jo

Kopechne have thought of Ted's career?" Its conclusion: "maybe she'd feel it was worth it."

Mary Jo Kopechne had become an abortion martyr.

———

American feminism is not a blue-collar phenomenon. Almost all of its most prominent figures come from elite backgrounds. Gloria Steinem, the founder of *Ms.* magazine, went to Smith. Cecile Richards, the longtime head of Planned Parenthood, went to Brown. Her mother was the governor of Texas. Facebook COO Sheryl Sandberg is worth more than $1 billion and went to Harvard. Roxane Gay's parents came from Haiti, so she was hired by the *New York Times*, adding diversity to its large stable of feminist opinion writers. But Gay herself went to boarding school at Phillips Exeter. The next time you see someone making the feminist case on television, you can be confident she's not a former home health aide with a community college degree.

Not surprisingly, affluent feminists tend to lack perspective on oppression. Some speak as if the cruelest fate that can befall a woman is to be patronized by a man, or trapped in a soulless suburb doing laundry and microwaving dinner. But in the world beyond Santa Monica, there are greater threats to women.

Imagine a place where women are punished for being raped. A place where women are murdered for having affairs. Where women lack equal access to basic health care, and not just abortions. Where women can't use public swimming pools, and are required to have a male guardian, without whose permission they cannot travel, obtain a passport, or even get married.

This is not a Margaret Atwood novel. It's a real place called Saudi Arabia, one of America's most significant military allies and a major sponsor of conservative Islam worldwide. In Saudi Arabia, every woman is subject to the authority of a "wali," a male guardian who is typically her husband, father, or other family member. Women require the wali's permission to do almost anything of importance, and a woman who disobeys her wali can be imprisoned.

Other countries governed by Islamic law and customs follow similar principles, distinguished only by a greater level of violence.

In 2016, a social media celebrity named Qandeel Baloch was strangled to death by her brother in an apparent honor killing in the Pakistani state of Punjab. Her crime? Posting pictures of herself online. It was one of at least one thousand honor killings in Pakistan that year, and every year.

In most cases the perpetrators are never punished, possibly because they enjoyed wide community support. A 2014 survey by Pew Research found that more than 40 percent of all Pakistanis believe honor killings are justified if the killing involves a woman who engaged in premarital sex or adultery.

These attitudes travel. London, home to high numbers of Pakistani immigrants, recorded more than eleven thousand "honor crimes" between 2010 and 2014, including eighteen murders.

In 2006, a reporter for the *Guardian* visited a genital mutilation ceremony in Indonesia, an annual event held every year on the lunar anniversary of Muhammad's birthday. Hundreds of girls, some infants, lay on desks at a local school and waited to have their genitals mutilated with scissors. A local Islamic organization sponsored the event. For every daughter they brought, parents received seven dollars and a bag of food.

"It is necessary to control women's sexual urges," the event's organizer explained to the *Guardian.* "They must be chaste to preserve their beauty."

Attitudes like this are common in the Muslim world. The UN estimates that about 200 million girls have undergone genital mutilation, including virtually every woman in Somalia.

Thanks to mass immigration, these customs have arrived in the United States. In 2017, three Muslim immigrants from India were arrested for running a female genital mutilation ring out of six medical clinics across Michigan. At trial, prosecutors estimated that as many as one hundred girls may have undergone clitorectomies.

Honor killings, too, are now a feature of American life. In July 2008, a Pakistani man living in the suburbs of Atlanta strangled his twenty-five-year-old daughter with a bungee cord because she wanted to end an arranged marriage. Speaking through an Urdu translator at his arraignment, the father declared, "I have done nothing wrong."

In 2014, an Iraqi immigrant in El Cajon, California, was convicted of beating his wife to death because she wanted a divorce. A 2015 study submitted to the Department of Justice estimated that there are dozens of honor killings in the United States every year by immigrants, virtually all of them of women who have become "too Westernized."

Attitudes like this pose a threat not just to immediate family, but to the wider society. Migration from the Islamic world has led to a wave of sex crimes in Europe. During New Year's Eve celebrations in Germany at the end of 2015, hundreds of women in Cologne were groped and sexually assaulted in public by mobs of men, almost entirely of Arab or North African origin. Stunningly, the police initially reacted by ignoring the attacks entirely, bothering to investigate only after widespread complaints on social media exposed the cover-up.

In the British city of Rotherham, a group of Pakistani men abducted, sexually abused, and raped more than 1,400 children, primarily teenage girls, for more than a decade. Police and local government knew about the crimes, but did nothing. Officials feared that singling out the Muslim community for investigation would be decried as racist.

Rotherham was merely the largest case of such abuse in the United Kingdom. Similar long-running abuse rings involving dozens of Muslim men have been uncovered in Rochdale, Bristol, Derby, Halifax, Keighly, Newcastle, Oxford, and Aylesbury.

You'd guess that feminists would see traditional Islamic views of women, and the increasing prevalence of those views in the West, as a serious concern. The importation of medieval customs from the Islamic world is likely the most significant threat to the social advances women have made since the 1960s. Women's groups should be sounding the alarm. They're not.

"Immigration is a feminist issue," declares NOW's website. Erecting barriers to immigration is part of "an agenda fueled by racism" and "driven by hate," the group says. NOW's argument has been repeated robotically by every large feminist organization.

"Why Immigration Is a Feminist Issue," reads a 2011 headline in the *Nation*. In 2013, an identical headline appeared on Every dayFeminism.com. A 2016 column in the *Guardian* declared the flood of migrants entering Europe from Africa and the Middle East to be a feminist issue, and not in the sense that women would need protection from a group that is disproportionately young, aggressive men with retrograde attitudes about gender roles.

Remarkably, feminists have attacked women who criticize

traditional Islamic views of women. In 2017, writers Ayaan Hirsi Ali and Asra Nomani traveled to Washington to testify before a Senate committee. Both had been born into Muslim households, Nomani in India and Ali in Somalia, where she was the victim of genital mutilation. Both later became Westernized liberals. Nomani campaigns for feminism within Islam while Ali, now an atheist, published a book calling for a wholesale reformation of the religion. While in Washington, the two wanted to talk about the threat Islamic customs pose to women around the world. Feminist leaders weren't interested.

At the hearing, Senator Kamala Harris of California snubbed both of the women entirely, refusing even to ask questions. "We believe feminism is for everyone," Ali and Nomani wrote later. "Our goals—not least the equality of the sexes—are deeply liberal. We know these are values that the Democratic senators at our hearing share. Will they find their voices and join us in opposing Islamist extremism and its war on women?"

For now, the answer is no. The 2017 Women's March on Washington might have been a useful time to mention the millions of women around the world oppressed by Islamic regimes. Instead, organizers adopted as their motif a picture of a Muslim woman wearing an Islamic headscarf, perhaps the most familiar symbol of men's control over women in the Islamic world.

Cochairing the march was Linda Sarsour, a Muslim American separatist who not only wears a hijab but has vocally defended the sharia codes under which women around the world are oppressed. In 2011, Sarsour remarked that Ayaan Hirsi Ali didn't deserve to be a woman and should have her vagina taken away as punishment, presumably in addition to the genital mutilation Ali had already endured as a child.

None of this bothered professional feminists. During the Obama administration, Sarsour was celebrated on the White House website as a "champion of change." *Time* magazine added her to its list of the one hundred most influential people. New York senator Kirsten Gillibrand described Sarsour as "one of the suffragists of our time."

———

One of the most influential books in recent years is Sheryl Sandberg's *Lean In*, a guide to empowerment for women in the workplace. Published in 2013, *Lean In* sold more than two million copies and spawned a nonprofit foundation that organizes support groups for professional women around the world. Sandberg lays out her thesis in the book's introduction: "A truly equal world would be one where women ran half our countries and companies and men ran half our homes," she writes. "I believe that this would be a better world."

Sandberg's words are invariably characterized as a vision of equality, but that's not quite what they are. What Sandberg is describing is sameness, a world where men and women are interchangeable parts, like widgets in a bin awaiting assembly. That's not a surprising view from a corporate chieftain. Sandberg goes on to say that if men and women were exactly the same, "our collective performance would improve." Earnings would rise, investors would profit. Ignoring gender differences would be an enormous boon to market capitalism. McKinsey studies prove that.

Profitable as it might be for companies like Sandberg's, this is an idea rooted in fantasy. The sexes are not the same. Over broad populations, men and women have different talents and different interests. That is not an opinion. It is scientifically observable, as well as the conclusion of any honest person who pays attention. The differences are real. Pretending they're not doesn't change reality. Forcing an entire society to lie about the nature of men and women is bound to cause enormous problems. And it has.

If you spent decades punishing anyone who acknowledged inherent sex differences, transgender politics is what you'd wind up with. The core belief in transgenderism is that biology isn't real: sex is not determined at the DNA level; it's determined by appearance. If you look like a man, you're a man. If you look like a woman, you're a woman. You are what you say you are, even if it's a description you invented yourself. Anyone who doubts you must be fired.

It's a measure of how bovine our ruling class has become that educated people fall for nonsense like this especially hard. Employees of Facebook came up with more than seventy gender choices for their site. The choices include asexual, gender neutral, polygender, agender, bigender, gender fluid, gender variant, neutrois, pangender, transmasculine, as well as something called two-spirit, which one noted expert on gender identity described, unhelpfully, as "a sacred, spiritual and ceremonial role that is recognized and confirmed by the Elders of the Two Spirit's ceremonial community."

There's not a person on earth who could define all of these categories. Some of them don't really have definitions. It doesn't matter. Their legitimacy is defended with determined ruthlessness by the arbiters of gender politics.

In 2015 at UCLA, the student newspaper issued an apology for publishing an article that associated menstruation with women. As the paper pointed out, not everyone who menstruates is a woman, and not everyone who is a woman can menstruate. That same year, all-women Mount Holyoke College canceled a performance of *The Vagina Monologues*. Associating women with the possession of a vagina, students decided, was hurtful and exclusionary.

Nothing in science supports these views. A 2013 study in the *Journal of the American Academy of Child and Adolescent Psychiatry* found that two-thirds of children who say they believe they were born the wrong gender change their minds and come to accept their biological sex. Another study, by clinical psychologist Devita Singh, found that without adult intervention, 88 percent of kids ultimately evolve out of gender confusion.

Feminists have ignored these findings and continue to push for transition treatments for young children. In Canada, psychologist Ken Zucker was fired, and had his Gender Identity Clinic closed, because he argued that most children shouldn't begin the sometimes irreversible process of gender transition.

You don't have to think too far ahead to see the potential threats to biological women from this ideology. Locker rooms, bathrooms, and public showers are segregated by sex primarily to protect women, who by nature of their physical design are more susceptible to sexual assault than men are.

Many sports are also segregated by sex, and this is also a response to biology. On average, thanks to nature, men have greater physical size and strength. It wouldn't be fair to have women compete with men in most contests. Without the WNBA, a sex-segregated league, not a single woman would be able to play professional basketball. Again, acknowledging sex differences protects women.

If any of this has occurred to professional feminists, nobody's saying it out loud. Instead women's groups have decided to embrace the transgender movement, apparently on the grounds that every new advance in human sexuality is positive. But, as of 2018, it's still not entirely clear what transgenderism is, much less what the rules are.

Consider this explanation from Planned Parenthood, an organization that describes itself as the final word in sex education for young women. Read it twice and see if you can understand what it means:

> Passing describes the experience of a transgender person being seen by others as the gender they want to be seen as. An example would be a trans woman using the women's bathroom and being seen as female by those around her. Passing is extremely important for many transgender people. Passing can be emotionally important because it affirms your gender identity. Passing can also provide safety from harassment and violence. Because of transphobia, a transgender person who passes may experience an easier time moving through the world than a person who is known to be transgender or looks more androgynous. But not all transgender people feel the same way about passing. While passing is important to some people, others feel the word suggests that some people's gender presentation isn't as real as others. They may feel that passing implies that being seen by others as cisgender is more important than being known as transgender. Some transgender people are comfortable with and proud to be out as trans and don't feel the need to pass as a cisgender person.

Got that? A man dressed as a woman demands to be treated as a woman, except in cases where that would be patronizing, at which point he demands to be seen as a man dressing as a woman. But in every circumstance, he is proudly transgender. Or something to that effect. The rules are evolving as we watch.

So are the consequences. In many big cities and almost every college campus, no grounds exist for keeping a man out of a women's locker room, provided he claims to identify as a woman. The predictable abuses have already started to happen.

In 2016, in Seattle, a man entered a women's locker room at a public pool while young girls were changing. When confronted by staff, the man pointed out that he had the right to be treated as his preferred gender and couldn't be told to leave. Under the laws of the city of Seattle, endorsed by feminist groups, he was right.

Maybe the greatest irony of feminist-endorsed transgenderism is that it threatens to undo the achievements of Title IX, a 1972 law banning sex discrimination in public education. Feminists are proud of Title IX and the vast athletic opportunities for women it created. Thanks to the law, American girls have more teams to play on than girls in any other country in the world.

Yet now, in the United States and in international competitions, biological men who identify as women can compete as female athletes, despite the immense biological advantages they enjoy even after undergoing hormone treatments.

Not surprisingly, men have performed well against their biologically female competitors. In 2017, a biological man won multiple girls' titles at Connecticut's state track-and-field meet. Cyclist Jill Bearden (born Jonathan) almost immediately became a top-tier female cyclist once he transitioned, winning El Tour de Tucson in 2016. In New Zealand, transgender weight lifter Laurel Hubbard has smashed multiple records with ease after making a gender switch.

Instead of lamenting that a women's sport is being dominated by a biological man, a representative of New Zealand's
weight-lifting organization called Hubbard "tremendously cou-
rageous" for competing against women. Hubbard won't be the
last man to displace female competitors from women's athletic
events.

———

Men posing as female weight lifters isn't the biggest problem
Western civilization faces, but it's an ominous symptom of
deeper rot. When the people in charge retreat into fantasy, and
demand that everyone else join them there, society itself becomes
impervious to reality. The entire population develops the habits
of fact-avoidance and lying. After a while, nobody can see a crisis,
or even admit one exists.

This has happened with the crisis of men in America, which
is both real and largely ignored. If you're a middle-aged American man, you probably know at least one peer who has killed
himself in recent years, and maybe more than one. If you're a
parent, you may have noticed that your daughter's friends seem
more impressive than your son's. They get better grades. They
smoke less weed. They go to more prestigious colleges. If you're
an employer, you may have noticed that your female employees
show up on time. The young men often don't. And of course
if you live in America, you've seen a horrifying series of mass
shootings, far more than the country has ever had. In every case,
the shooter was a man.

Something awful is happening to men in America. What's
odd is how rarely you hear it publicly acknowledged. Our leaders
pledge to create more opportunities for women and girls, who

they imply are failing. The opposite is true. Thanks to intimidation from a relatively small group of influential feminists, nobody can admit it.

The average American man dies five years before the average American woman. One of the reasons for this is addiction. Men are more than twice as likely as women to become alcoholics. They're also twice as likely to die of a drug overdose. In New Hampshire, one of the states hit hardest by the opioid crisis, 73 percent of overdose deaths were men.

But the saddest reason for shortened life spans is suicide. Seventy-seven percent of all suicides are committed by men. The overall rate is increasing at a dramatic pace. Between 1999 and 2014, there was a 43 percent rise in suicide deaths among middle-aged American men.

You often hear of America's incarceration crisis. That's almost exclusively a male problem, too. More than 90 percent of inmates are men.

These problems are complex, and they start young. Relative to girls, boys are failing in school. More girls than boys graduate high school. Considerably more go to and graduate from college. Boys account for the overwhelming majority of school discipline cases. One study found that fully one in five high school boys had been diagnosed with hyperactivity disorder, compared with just one in eleven girls. Many were medicated for it. The long-term health effects of those medications aren't fully understood, but they appear to include depression in later life.

Women decisively outnumber men in graduate school. They earn the majority of doctoral degrees. They are now the majority of new enrollees in both law and medical schools.

For men, the consequences of failing in school are lifelong.

Between 1979 and 2010, working-age men with only high school degrees saw their real hourly wages drop about 20 percent. Over the same period, high-school-educated women saw their wages rise. The decline of the industrial economy disproportionately hurt men.

About seven million American men between the ages of twenty-five and fifty-four no longer have jobs. That's more than 10 percent of the entire working-age male labor force in the United States. Nearly half of these men take pain medication on any given day, the highest rate in the world. Most of them, researchers predict, will never return to work.

Some of the causes of this are well known. Competition from lower-priced foreign labor crushed America's manufacturing sector. China's entry into the World Trade Organization alone destroyed more than two million American jobs. Automation is killing many more. A disproportionate number of these jobs are in traditionally male industries: manufacturing, agriculture, logging. One 2016 report found that "90 percent of what welders, cutters, solderers, and brazers do" could be replaced by robots.

Jobs in which women are the majority tend to be far less vulnerable to automation. Three of the five fastest-growing professions are dominated by women. The jobs that remain for men tend to pay far less than the ones that disappeared.

As a consequence of this decline, far fewer young men get married than did just a few decades ago, and fewer stay married. About one in five American children live with only their mothers. That's double the rate in 1970. Millions more boys are growing up without fathers. Young adult men are now more likely to live with a parent than with a spouse or partner. That is not the case for young women.

Men are even falling behind physically. A recent study found that almost half of young men failed the army's entry-level physical fitness test during basic training. Fully 70 percent of American men are overweight or obese, as compared to 59 percent of American women.

Perhaps most terrifyingly, men seem to be becoming less male. Sperm counts across the West have plummeted, down almost 60 percent since the early 1970s. Scientists don't know why. Testosterone levels in men have also fallen precipitously. One study found that the average levels of male testosterone dropped by 1 percent every year after 1987. This is unrelated to age. The average forty-year-old man in 2017 would have testosterone levels 30 percent lower than the average forty-year-old man in 1987.

There is no upside to this. Lower testosterone levels in men are associated with depression, lethargy, weight gain, and decreased cognitive ability. Nothing like this has ever happened. You'd think the country would want to know what exactly is going on and how to fix it. But policy makers and the media ignore the story. It's considered a fringe topic.

Nor is it a priority in the scientific research establishment. There are virtually no NIH-funded studies on why testosterone levels are falling. The federal government has funded research on "Pubic Hair Grooming Prevalence and Motivation Among Women in the United States."

Feminists scoff at the notion of a crisis among men, but ignoring it doesn't help anyone. Men and women need each other. One cannot exist without the other. When men fail, everyone suffers.

Consider the broader effects of low male wages. Whenever gender differences come up in public debate, the so-called wage gap dominates the conversation. A woman makes 77 cents for every dollar a man earns. The statistic is repeated everywhere. But that number compares all American men to all American women across all professions. No legitimate social scientist would consider that a valid measure. The number is both meaningless and intentionally misleading. It's a talking point.

Once you compare men and women with similar experience working the same hours in similar jobs for the same period of time—and that's the only way you can measure it—the gap all but disappears. In fact it may invert. One study using census data found that single women in their twenties living in metropolitan areas now earn 8 percent more on average than their male counterparts.

Millions of American men make less than their fathers did. This is a depressing betrayal of the American dream, but it's also a recipe for societal collapse. When men's wages decline, families fall apart. This fact is well known to researchers. It's been the subject of many studies over decades, with consistent results. One study released in 2017 found that when men's wages fell relative to women's, young people stopped getting married. According to the authors, a falling male wage reduced "the attractiveness of men as potential spouses, thus reducing fertility and especially marriage rates."

Researchers also noted a dramatic increase in out-of-wedlock births when men made less. In the words of one of the authors, an economics professor at MIT, "We see a decline in fertility, a decline in marriage, but a rise in the fraction of births that are disadvantaged, and as a consequence the kids are living in pretty tough circumstances."

Numerous academic studies have reached identical conclusions. Research from 2015 found that "when a randomly chosen woman becomes more likely to earn more than a randomly chosen man, marriage rates decline." Those who do marry report being less satisfied and are more likely to divorce.

Low male wages are a driving force in family dissolution. That's why affluent neighborhoods in which men make more have a higher proportion of married couples, and fewer divorces. The opposite is also true, and that leads to a cascade of social problems, which over time become a disaster: Men who make lower wages marry less and father more children out of wedlock. These children, growing up without fathers, tend to make lower wages themselves in later life.

For decades this was a universally recognized pattern in inner cities: the cycle of poverty. Now the same destructive vortex is common in rural America. In both cases, the cause is the same: a lack of well-paying jobs for men.

A society filled with idle men is an unstable society. At best, it's a sad place. Men need to work or they fall apart. Work is central to a man's identity in a way that it is not for the average woman. Terrified of violating feminist orthodoxy, policy makers can't say this out loud, or respond accordingly. Instead a decadent ruling class rationalizes away the ways in which it has failed men by constructing fantasies about a future world, one where mass male unemployment will be a sign of success.

In 2015, a journalist named Derek Thompson wrote a much-discussed piece in the *Atlantic* titled "A World Without Work." Someday, Thompson predicted, "the 20th century will strike future historians as an aberration, with its religious devotion to overwork in a time of prosperity, its attenuations of family in service to job opportunity, its conflation of income with self-worth."

Elites in Washington loved the piece. They were particularly grateful for Thompson's optimism about the collapse of manufacturing jobs in places like Youngstown, Ohio. Thompson found one former factory worker who, at sixty, got a new job as a teacher. Repeated cycles of unemployment, Thompson suggested, were in fact enabling self-actualization.

This is not how previous generations of leaders responded to the crisis of male unemployment. Just two months after his inauguration in 1933, Franklin Roosevelt presented Congress with a response to the unprecedented joblessness of the Great Depression. Roosevelt proposed a government employment program for unmarried young men called the Civilian Conservation Corps. Its workforce would not compete with established industries, FDR promised, but would instead confine itself "to forestry, the prevention of soil erosion, flood control and similar projects."

The work of the CCC was designed to be useful to the country, but that wasn't the main point. Just a year before, FDR's predecessor Herbert Hoover had been forced to deploy soldiers to disperse jobless World War I veterans who were marching menacingly on Washington. Roosevelt understood how dangerous millions of unemployed men could be.

Congress approved the idea immediately. Within three months, a quarter of a million men were enrolled in the CCC, living in tents in camps around the country. Only the military had the logistical ability to pull off mobilization this complex, so FDR put General Douglas MacArthur in charge.

Over the next nine years, the CCC transformed the landscape of rural America. Its workers planted more than three billion trees. They fought forest and prairie fires, built 125,000 miles of roads and 13,000 miles of walking trails, strung 89,000 miles of phone lines. They built fish hatcheries and wildlife refuges, constructed cabins and stonework in hundreds of state parks.

About three million men passed through the CCC, waking up early for exercise six days a week, living a regimented life that was a mixture of the Boy Scouts and the army. Each man earned about $30 a month. In a nod to the reality that men are providers, men were required to send all but $5 home to their families. The majority of workers arrived in CCC camps malnourished. On average, they gained twelve pounds over the first year.

The CCC turned out to be the most popular government program of the Great Depression, with solid majorities of both Democrats and Republicans supporting it. It would be denounced as irredeemably sexist today.

In the face of evidence that men are falling behind, the stated aim of most politicians is to raise women's wages to parity or above men's. There's nothing inherently wrong with that. But it's notable that most women, the very population on whose behalf these policies are supposedly created, strongly prefer to marry men who make more than they do.

Meanwhile, a lot of Americans have stopped getting married. Once again this is a trend that hurts everyone, men, women, and children. Between 1960 and 2016, the proportion of children living with both parents decreased by almost 20 percent. The percentage of children living with only their mothers nearly tripled. In demographic terms, this is stunning. Changes to family structure this abrupt are rarely seen in peacetime.

Yet if anything, those numbers understate the reality of fatherlessness in America. In high-income neighborhoods, not much has changed. Most kids grow up with their mothers and fathers. But in the rest of the country, intact families are disappearing.

According to a 2014 study by researchers at Johns Hopkins University, among younger parents without college degrees, "74 percent of the mothers and 70 percent of the fathers had at least one child outside of marriage." Out-of-wedlock births are now the rule across the country, not the exception.

Increasingly, having a father at home is a sign of affluence. But it is also a cause of affluence, especially for boys. Boys who grow up with a father at home earn much more as adults. Boys who grow up alone with their mothers tend to earn less. They also have more disciplinary problems in school. They read less, and less well. They're less likely to graduate from high school or go to college. They are more likely to be unemployed and to live in poverty. They get married less often, and when they do, they divorce more. They're more likely to be obese and have asthma. They're far more likely to abuse alcohol and drugs, exhibit antisocial behavior, and commit acts of violence. As adults, they're twice as likely to go to prison.

Numerous longitudinal studies, done over generations, show the devastating effects of fatherlessness. The results hold true across geography and ethnic groups: white, black; urban, rural. Boys raised without their fathers are at serious risk. The nationwide breakup of families is a disaster, and not just a moral disaster, but a practical one. It is one of the largest public health problems the country faces.

When was the last time you heard an establishment figure decry the out-of-wedlock birthrate? Politics account for some of this. Unmarried mothers are a critical part of the Democratic coalition. In 2008, Barack Obama won 74 percent of single mothers who voted. In 2012, he won 75 percent. Alienating these voters is politically risky for Democrats. It's been more than twenty years since a Democrat running for president won the majority of married women in America. Unmarried women, by contrast, vote overwhelmingly for Democrats. The last Democratic platform to mention the importance of having a father at home was in 2000.

In 2013, as she was preparing to run for president, Hillary Clinton shot a video tribute to single mothers. "Single moms are real heroines," she said. "They need even more of the help that grandparents, aunts and uncles and good friends can provide." The one group that Hillary didn't mention: biological fathers.

Elites who stray from the script pay a price. Barack Obama spoke regularly and often eloquently about the importance of fatherhood. Yet he said almost nothing about men marrying the mothers of their children. That distinction is critical. Studies show that married fathers are by far the most involved in their children's lives. You often hear politicians refer to "caring parents, grandparents, and caregivers," or some similar combination, as if the presence of any involved adult were enough for kids. But that's not true. At least for boys, the presence of a biological father in the house makes all the difference.

On at least one occasion, Obama suggested he understood this. In 2013, during a speech in Chicago about gun violence, Obama noted that "we should do more to promote marriage."

Almost immediately, professional feminists complained. An article in *Ebony* magazine suggested Obama's remarks were bigoted. MSNBC ran an op-ed attacking him. And so on. Obama went back to platitudes.

Mostly, he stayed there. In March 2009, almost immediately after arriving in Washington, Obama created the White House Council on Women and Girls, and tapped his advisor Valerie Jarrett to run it. "When our daughters don't have the same education and career opportunities as our sons," Obama said in his announcement, "that affects our economy and our future as a nation."

You'd have to ignore an enormous amount of research data to repeat the pieties of 1970s-era feminism, but Obama did. At the very moment he was lamenting the lack of educational opportunities for women, more girls than boys were graduating from high school. Far more were graduating from college. Women now earn 62 percent of associate's degrees, 57 percent of bachelor's degrees, 60 percent of master's degrees, and 52 percent of doctorates.

The gap is even wider in nonwhite neighborhoods. Among black and Hispanic graduates of Boston public schools, for example, for every 100 boys who went to college from the class of 2007, there were 186 girls. Seventy percent of all master's degrees awarded to black students nationally went to black women. Just 30 percent went to black men. Yet, for reasons the Obama administration never explained, the school performance of black and Hispanic girls was deemed a higher priority than the performance of black and Hispanic boys.

Under Obama, the White House solicited hundreds of millions of dollars from corporations to encourage female achievement in higher education. At the time this was happening, one study showed that there were already at least four times as many privately funded college scholarships available for girls as for boys.

The administration never acknowledged any of this. Instead it sought new ways to close a gender gap that no longer existed. One idea, imported directly from feminist intellectuals: "breaking down gender stereotypes in toys." The White House pressured manufacturers, retailers, and media outlets to eliminate gender distinctions in children's toys. This, the administration claimed, would allow kids "to explore, learn, and dream without limits."

Educators at all levels took this idea seriously. In 2015, one kindergarten teacher in Washington State banned her male students from playing with Legos. Fitting together plastic blocks has been found to help children develop important cognitive skills. Boys have enough advantages, the teacher explained. So she intentionally prevented them from learning.

Girls thrive when boys fail. This is the underlying assumption of modern feminism, and it's reflected in education policy, especially on college campuses. The irony is remarkable.

There are more than two million more women than men enrolled in American colleges. On most campuses, men are a distinct minority. At Carlow University in Pittsburgh, women outnumber men by more than six to one. Yet almost every campus has a women's studies department. In many of them, the stated goal is to fight expressions of masculinity and disempower men.

At Ohio State, a course began in the spring of 2018 called "Be a Man! Masculinities, Race and Nation." The syllabus explained that masculinity is used to "justify certain kinds of violence by men." On the first day of class, students were required to consult a "male privilege checklist."

At Duke, a nine-week workshop met to devise ways to undermine "masculinity and maleness, as well as to create destabilized spaces for those with privilege," meaning men. Similar projects sprouted at colleges all over the country.

Under the Obama administration, the Department of Justice created something called the Healthy Masculinity Campus Athletics Project. The coordinator of the program at Wheaton

College summed up the objective this way: "as a country, we need to do a better job of addressing issues around toxic masculinity."

Left unasked was the most basic question: Is masculinity itself really toxic? And what happens to boys when we tell them it is?

It is widely understood that attacking people for their basic nature is unhealthy and wrong. A government-funded program designed to fight "toxic femininity" or "toxic homosexuality" probably wouldn't escape the scrutiny of Congress or the media. At the very least, its supporters would have to explain why the country needs a program like that. Yet nobody's been forced to explain why boys, who are already failing, need to be held back further.

The small group of unhappy people in charge of America's gender policies don't want to talk about it. So nobody does.

SEVEN

They Don't Pick Up Trash Anymore

I f you're over forty and grew up in the United States, you
probably remember the crying-Indian ad. It was one of the
longest-running public service advertisements of all time,
ubiquitous during the 1970s. It seemed to air in every commercial break during *Gilligan's Island* as my brother and I watched
after school. It got me every time.

The spot opens with a weathered American Indian man
in buckskins paddling a birchbark canoe down the middle of
a stream lined with trees. It's a peaceful tableau, and the man
looks serene in his regal Indian way.

Suddenly ominous music comes up in the background. A
piece of trash floats past the bow of the canoe. It's jarringly out of
place, like a cockroach on a cake. It's repulsive.

Then the camera pulls back. Behind the Indian is an enormous steel power plant, pouring smoke into the sky. The man pulls his canoe onto the shore, which is covered with beer bottles and food wrappers, and begins to walk. Soon he's standing by the side of a busy highway. Cars roar by.

The narration begins: "Some people have a deep, abiding respect for the natural beauty that was once this country. . . . And some people don't."

With that, a man in a speeding white Impala throws a paper sack of half-eaten fast food from his car window. It lands at the Indian's feet and explodes, covering his moccasins with soggy French fries. The camera tightens on the Indian's face. A single tear rolls slowly down his cheek.

"People start pollution," says the narrator. "People can stop it."

It was emotionally exhausting to watch. Not only did you feel terrible for the Indian, who was hit with garbage, but you truly hated the guy in the Impala and everyone like him. Americans inherited the prettiest natural landscape in the world, and they spoiled it. Because some people are stupid and greedy, the air is brown and the streams are clogged with trash. Morons toss their refuse out of car windows. Wildlife dies. Indians cry. It was awful.

But it was also fixable. There was nothing abstract about the solution to this disaster: Stop being selfish and messy. Pick up your garbage. Clean up your country. It's a beautiful place. Don't wreck it.

This was environmentalism a first grader could understand. It was a conservation ethic designed to improve the lives of living things, people and animals. The message was dire but not hopeless. It made you want to pick up trash.

The ad made the crying Indian a national celebrity. His

name was Iron Eyes Cody. He died in 1999 at the age of ninety-four in Los Angeles. He probably thought he had made a difference.

In 2018, the city of Los Angeles counted 55,188 homeless people on its streets, 75 percent of them living in the open air. Across the city the homeless were passed out on sidewalks, sleeping on benches, camped out in parks. They were relieving themselves everywhere.

On skid row, there were a total of nine toilets for the almost two thousand people believed to be sleeping in the area. Many people just dropped their pants in the street. Andy Bales, head of the Union Rescue Mission in the neighborhood, told the *Guardian* that the area was so dirty, it posed a life-threatening health hazard. "I lost my leg because I got *E. coli* and staph and strep from the sidewalk because of feces being present," he said.

A 2012 survey of the neighborhood by the Los Angeles County Department of Public Health found "piles of feces and/or urine on the sidewalks and grass areas of the majority of the streets surveyed." Storm drains were clogged with human waste. There were discarded hypodermic needles on almost every block. A UN monitor visiting Los Angeles found filth "on a scale I hadn't anticipated."

But it was still cleaner than San Francisco. A survey by the local NBC station in the spring of 2018 found garbage strewn over all 153 blocks of downtown San Francisco. On more than forty blocks, there were discarded hypodermic needles. Close to one hundred blocks had piles of human feces. "The contamination," said an infectious disease specialist from UC Berkeley, is "much greater than communities in Brazil or Kenya or India."

But for scale, nothing beats the filth of New York City. In

2018, there were an estimated 76,000 homeless people living in New York. The *Daily News* described one abandoned rail bed in the South Bronx, located directly across the street from a school, as blanketed with used hypodermic needles: "There are needles scattered on the ground like twigs and needles clumped under trees like piles of leaves. Needles are staked into a mud wall. Needles are floating in the pools of standing water below. Some of the syringes' tips are still stained with blood."

It's not just New York, Los Angeles, and San Francisco. Dozens of U.S. cities tolerate record levels of homelessness, public drug use, and filth. America has become much dirtier in recent years. Whatever happened to the crying Indian?

Strangely, environmentalism as an idea is more popular than ever. Go to San Francisco and see for yourself. Walk through Sea Cliff or Presidio Heights or any affluent neighborhood in the city and ask the first five people you meet if they consider themselves environmentalists. If only four say yes, chances are the fifth doesn't speak English well enough to understand the question.

Just about everyone in elite America is an environmentalist. It's all but mandatory. What's changed is the definition of environmentalism. The new environmentalism has everything to do with making elites more powerful and self-satisfied. It has very little to do with improving the natural world. Modern environmentalists step over piles of garbage and human excrement on their way to save the planet.

The early conservationists would have stopped to clean up the street. The founders of the modern environmental movement spent a great deal of time outdoors. Teddy Roosevelt, who as president put hundreds of millions of acres of land under federal protection, spent years of his life in canoes and on horseback, hunting and fishing around the world. Aldo Leopold, who helped to found the Wilderness Society in the 1930s, once worked for the Forest Service in the then-territory of New Mexico, where his job included shooting bears and mountain lions. John Muir, who founded the Sierra Club, lived alone for years in Yosemite in a cabin he built himself, working as a shepherd. These were people who knew the difference between a conifer and a deciduous tree, who could name three bird species and identify a brook trout and never confuse deer with caribou. They became naturalists because they loved nature.

The early environmental movement reflected their outlook. Environmental groups preserved wilderness, created the national parks, fought pollution, and successfully lobbied for clean air and water legislation. The issues were straightforward. The goals were measurable.

Over time, environmentalists improved America. Waterways are far cleaner than they were in the 1970s. Ecosystems and fisheries have been restored, land has been preserved, and birds of prey are flourishing rather than at risk of extinction.

I watched it firsthand as a kid on the Androscoggin River in Maine, where I spent summers canoeing and fishing. For generations, paper mills dumped toxic effluent in the river. The water turned unnatural colors and smelled bad. The trout died. The water was not just undrinkable, but considered dangerous to touch. Locals claimed it peeled the paint off houses near the riverbank.

You didn't have to work at Greenpeace to find this offensive. The paper companies didn't own the river. They had no right to destroy it. But until Congress passed the Clean Water Act, they did it anyway. Now the river is clean enough to bathe in, and the trout have returned. It's a huge improvement. The environmental movement deserves credit for that.

The problem is, there are only so many rivers you can restore before you run out of high-profile victories. At that point, where does your movement go? And more pressing for the thousands of professional activists with children and mortgages, how do you raise money?

A few months after Obama's election, a friend of mine and I rented an office on Dupont Circle in Washington. We found the place on Craigslist. It was being sublet by an environmental group that was moving to new space in a more expensive part of town. One of the employees showed us around before we moved in. Two of the sinks in the office, he conceded, didn't really work. What's wrong with them? I asked.

With remarkably little embarrassment, he told me. "We repainted the inside of the office and then poured the paint down the sinks and it clogged them," he said.

You poured paint down a sink? Aren't you an environmental group? "Yeah," he said, "we shouldn't have done that." He didn't seem very concerned about it.

Within days, he was gone, off to enjoy his new office, a shiny glass and steel space with working sinks. The group was suddenly flush with cash. They'd just won a multiyear grant to work on climate change.

With every passing year, the goals of the environmental movement become steadily more abstract. Environmentalists have shifted their focus from the tangible world, with its feces-covered sidewalks septic enough to infect pedestrians with *E. coli*, to concerns invisible to the naked eye, or even to science. Environmentalists now spend a lot of their energy trying to solve purely theoretical problems. These battles can never be won, which is of course their main appeal. Meanwhile, the trash is piling up.

Ocean Beach is a narrow strip of national parkland along the western edge of San Francisco. In 2015, the National Park Service removed all trash cans from along the beach's seawall. Nobody announced the change, or solicited the opinions of beachgoers. One day, the trash cans just disappeared. A spokesman later explained that officials were "hoping to save staff time." Emptying trash cans took hours.

Very soon, the beach became filthy. Large piles of garbage collected along the seawall, some of it left by the city's vast homeless population. The trash stank. Neighbors and visitors complained, but to no effect. Park Service employees did not consider polluted beaches a meaningful environmental concern. They did not replace the trash cans. They did continue to update their website, including an extensive video series on "climate change in national parks."

In 1962, biologist Rachel Carson published a book that redefined what the environmental movement could achieve. Carson had studied the effects of government pesticide use, in particular the use of the chemical DDT, and concluded it was harmful to human health and devastating to bird populations. Her book was called *Silent Spring*, a reference to the absence of birdsong she predicted if the pesticide spraying continued. The book was serialized in the *New Yorker* and soon became a bestseller. It was an unexpected achievement for a science-heavy treatment of agricultural policy.

Carson died of cancer not long after *Silent Spring* was published, but the book's effects rippled outward for decades. Carson's work inspired the creation of the Environmental Protection Agency in 1970. Two years later, Congress banned the nonemergency use of DDT. As Carson had promised, eagle and falcon populations began to recover.

Rachel Carson became an icon of the American environmental movement. Jimmy Carter awarded her a posthumous Presidential Medal of Freedom. Her image was featured on postage stamps. Two of her homes were designated historic monuments. An elementary school in Maryland was named after her. To this day, the Audubon Society sponsors the Rachel Carson Award, in honor of her work to save bird populations.

Given all this, it's remarkable to see birds of prey once again dying in large numbers. Chemical companies aren't killing them. Environmentalists are. In 2011, at the urging of environmental groups, the Obama U.S. Fish & Wildlife Service granted an exemption to industrial wind companies under the Bald and Golden Eagle Protection Act. For most Americans, killing an eagle, even accidentally, remains a felony punishable by up to two years in prison. Corporate wind farms can kill eagles with impunity.

And they do. Wind turbines destroy hundreds of bald eagles every year. That's in addition to more than a quarter million other birds of various species, including hawks, owls, and songbirds crushed by turbine blades. Some experts believe the actual number of dead birds is much higher, possibly in the millions.

Two years after granting its initial exemption, the Obama administration gave a power company in California legal protection in the event its wind farms killed California condors, a critically endangered species with a wild population of fewer than three hundred. For the first time in many decades, killing condors was legal, as long as they were killed by wind turbines.

In addition to thinning bird populations, wind farms had a devastating effect on bats, a species already decimated in North America by a mysterious disease called white-nose syndrome. Bats regularly mistake wind turbines for trees. Somewhere between 600,000 and 800,000 of them are caught in wind rotors each year, though some experts suggest that number is "probably conservative."

Deepwater wind turbines, meanwhile, kill untold numbers of aquatic animals. In 2017, experts concluded that noise pollution from offshore wind farms may cause the beaching of humpback whales. Fishermen in New York claim that wind turbines in Long Island Sound are destroying fisheries by altering the migratory patterns of certain fish.

These are real costs, measurable in the carcasses of dead animals, many of them endangered. To environmental groups, they mean nothing compared to the entirely theoretical benefit of wind power.

On August 16, 2016, an illegal immigrant from Mexico with a long criminal record named Angel Gilberto Garcia-Avalos drove out of bounds in California's Sequoia National Park and crashed his car. The accident ignited a patch of dead grass, which in turn sparked a forest fire that grew to 29,322 acres in size and incinerated a large percentage of the park.

Garcia-Avalos, a native of Michoacán who had just been released from a California jail after being charged with a felony, did nothing to summon help. Forest Service officials finally arrived and asked him if he knew how the fire had started. Garcia-Avalos lied and denied responsibility. He said his car had been stolen. As he said this, a methamphetamine pipe fell out of his pocket and onto the ground.

In the end, the fire burned for six weeks and cost taxpayers $61 million before it was contained. Six homes were leveled. Cities across two counties had to be evacuated. The blaze destroyed forty-five square miles of Sequoia National Park.

The fire was an environmental disaster. Environmental groups ignored it. The Sierra Club, which was founded to preserve "the forests and other natural features" of the very region the fire burned, didn't issue a single statement about it. The Environmental Defense Fund issued half a dozen press releases during the same period, none of which said a word about the fire. Greenpeace was silent, too.

As the blaze raged, billionaire environmentalist Tom Steyer, a California resident, sent dozens of tweets about everything from fruit pickers to new climate measures. He never mentioned the fire. The Sierra Nevadas burned, but America's environmental establishment pretended nothing had happened.

It wasn't the first time. Throughout the West, illegal immigrants have left a wake of environmental destruction. According to a report by the U.S. Government Accountability Office, illegal immigrants caused 40 percent of the forest fires on the Arizona–Mexico border between 2006 and 2010. In many cases, the fires were deliberately set to mislead Border Patrol agents. In other cases, the fires started because of campfires or gunfire. The fires caused millions in economic damages. They also destroyed habitat for endangered species, increased the growth of nonnative plant species, and caused erosion.

A 2011 Interior Department study found that the Cabeza Prieta National Wildlife Refuge in Arizona, home to the last two hundred endangered Sonoran pronghorn left in the United States, had been marred by more than eight thousand miles of vehicle tracks left by drug and human smugglers. The report noted that constant illegal traffic was having a damaging effect on the plants, animals, and soil quality of the refuge.

In California, gangs of Mexican nationals have opened industrial marijuana farming operations on protected land throughout the state. An account in the *Los Angeles Times* describes "filthy work camps with makeshift kitchens, latrines and trash dumps in areas designated as wilderness. Biologists report fish die-offs and water contamination from fertilizers, pesticides and poisons used by growers."

The response from the environmental establishment to these threats to the environment? Demands for even more illegal immigration. In the fall of 2017, the Trump administration announced it was bowing to lawsuits from state attorneys general and ending the DACA program that granted amnesty to illegal immigrants.

The Environmental Defense Fund immediately issued a florid statement decrying the decision. "Environmental Defense Fund has no expertise in immigration policy," the group conceded with heavy understatement. "But we know that progress toward cleaner air and water is put at risk when the public debate is consumed by fear. . . . We will not ignore attacks on those who live around us. Their progress is ours."

Earthjustice, an organization of environmentalist attorneys, agreed. The group called the repeal of DACA a "senseless and spiteful attack on the fundamental principles of freedom, opportunity, and success."

The Sierra Club took a similar position. "The immigrant rights and environmental movements' concerns are intertwined," the group declared. "Those communities most threatened by Trump's presidency—immigrants, communities of color, and women—are also most vulnerable to toxic pollution and climate change."

None of these groups made a serious attempt to tie the repeal of DACA to actual environmental concerns. The Sierra Club didn't try to explain how secure borders cause "toxic pollution" or climate change. It wasn't necessary. Their donors understood the point: good people support the environment, oppose Trump, and protect illegal immigrants. They don't need to hear rational arguments about cause and effect.

The Sierra Club, which was formed to maintain hiking trails in Yosemite, now takes a vigorous position in favor of transgenderism and taxpayer-funded abortion. Its website includes a section on "Equity, Inclusion, and Justice," with articles like "Silence Is Consent: Solidarity with All People Fighting Oppression." In the summer of 2017, the Sierra Club signaled its opposition to the "unsustainable whiteness" of environmentalism.

Environmental racism is a longtime theme at the Sierra Club. The term first became popular at the tail end of the traditional environmental movement, when it was clear that the last of America's dirty rivers was finally getting clean. The concept was the brainchild of Robert Bullard, an energetic nonscientist with a degree in sociology. Bullard has written more than a dozen books on the topic, all with memorable titles, including *The Wrong Complexion for Protection*, *Residential Apartheid*, and *Dumping in Dixie*. Naturally, he is a favorite of television bookers.

In an interview with *Earth First! Journal*, Bullard explained that the fight against environmental racism isn't directly related to the environment. Instead, it is "more of a concept of trying to address power imbalances, lack of political enfranchisement, and to redirect resources so that we can create some healthy, livable and sustainable types of models."

Redirecting resources has always been a major part of it. In March 1990, dozens of self-described civil rights leaders wrote an open letter to the heads of America's ten biggest environmental groups accusing them of "racist and genocidal practices." The letter claimed that although environmentalists "often claim to represent our interests, in observing your activities it has become clear to us that your organizations play an equal role in the disruption of our communities." The proposed remedy: cash payments.

It's not clear who got paid how much, but by 2013 the Sierra Club and Robert Bullard were on excellent terms. The group gave Bullard one of its highest awards.

That same year, Obama EPA administrator Gina McCarthy told the Congressional Black Caucus that combating environmental racism was her agency's "core issue." McCarthy later explained that EPA regulations purportedly aimed at climate were really about "justice" for "communities of color." The agency directed millions in grants to fight environmental racism. To explain its rationale, the EPA's website quoted Robert Bullard.

What does any of this have to do with clean air and water? Nothing, obviously. But that doesn't mean modern environmentalism doesn't serve a purpose or meet a need. As a theology, environmentalism speaks deeply to America's elites. Its moral absolutes affirm them, adding meaning to their otherwise secular world. The collapse of mainline Protestantism left

TUCKER CARLSON

a void in the hearts of America's ruling class. The environmental movement fills it.

Seen this way, the movement's new priorities make sense. Environmentalism as a religion is more compelling than environmentalism as a means to save birds or clean up some river in Maine. After a while, details about the natural world begin to seem irrelevant. Compared to questions of virtue and salvation, they're not that interesting.

Leonardo DiCaprio understands this. DiCaprio is both a famous actor and perhaps the world's best-known climate activist. He doesn't speak on the subject of carbon emissions so much as he preaches. "Humans have put our entire existence into jeopardy," DiCaprio thunders. Climate change is "the most urgent threat facing our entire species." Those who question climate policy, he declares, should be banned from public office. "The scientific consensus is in, and the argument is now over."

Few preachers live up to the standards they set from the pulpit, and DiCaprio is no exception. In the summer of 2016, DiCaprio was scheduled to receive an award from the environmental group Riverkeeper. He was in Cannes attending the film festival at the time, so he chartered a private jet to fly from France to New York and back.

That's an eight-thousand-mile round-trip, which in addition to being physically exhausting, amounts to a gargantuan carbon footprint, bigger than the average African might emit in a lifetime. For DiCaprio, it was just another Cannes Film Festival. The year before, he was photographed off the coast of France meandering alone on the deck of a 450-foot, $200 million yacht, which he'd rented as an accommodation for the week. Once again, a lot of carbon.

Billionaire investor Richard Branson tells audiences not to "be the generation responsible for irreversibly damaging the environment" with carbon. To spread that message, he travels on his own Dassault Falcon 50EX. He also uses the plane when he flies to his private island in the Virgin Islands.

Like most billionaires, Bill Gates knows climate change is "a terrible problem, and it absolutely needs to be solved," but still flies on his Bombardier BD-700 Global Express. Same with fellow billionaire Elon Musk, who warns that climate change could lead to "more displacement and destruction than all the wars in history combined." Musk has a Gulfstream G650 ER.

Climate change crusader Hillary Clinton once demanded her own private plane because she didn't want to share one with Michelle Obama. Months after promising to put "a lot of coal miners and coal companies out of business" for their sins against the climate, Clinton flew twenty miles on a chartered jet from Martha's Vineyard to Nantucket for a fund-raiser with Cher.

On the last day of his presidency, Barack Obama took Air Force One from Washington, D.C., to a donor's house in California, an eleven-thousand-square-foot air-conditioned mansion in the middle of the hottest desert in North America. After a few days, Obama flew on Richard Branson's plane to a yacht that ferried him to Branson's island. A few weeks later, Obama hopped yet another private plane to French Polynesia, where he planned to write his memoirs on yet another private island, this one once owned by Marlon Brando.

New York mayor Bill de Blasio presides over an unusually dirty city, but the health of the environment is nevertheless vitally important to him. In 2017, he reminded radio listeners that "everyone in their own life has to change their own habits to start protecting the Earth." To show he meant it, de Blasio announced a number of new measures aimed at other people's behavior, including a ban on plastic bags in the city and a crackdown on idling vehicles.

When a caller pointed out that de Blasio takes a five-SUV motorcade from his Manhattan mansion to his gym in Brooklyn, he wistfully acknowledged that was true. "I wish my life was like everyone else's," he said, "but it's not, for obvious reasons." He added that it would be "cheap symbolism" for him to give up his many SUVs. And in any case, they're "fuel-efficient hybrids."

Al Gore is the closest thing America has to a climate saint, so it may seem odd that he often flies privately, and surprising that his house in Nashville uses twenty-one times the electricity of the average American home. Thankfully, the *New Republic* cleared that up. The magazine ran a piece titled "Al Gore's Carbon Footprint Doesn't Matter." The article attacked literal-minded conservatives for pointing to what was not actually hypocrisy at all.

Gore's office followed up with a response of its own: "Climate deniers, funded by the fossil fuel industry, continue to wage misleading personal attacks on Al Gore as a way of trying to cast doubt on established climate science and distract attention from the most serious global threat we face.

"Vice President Gore leads a carbon neutral life," the statement continued, "by purchasing green energy, reducing carbon impacts, and offsetting any emissions that cannot be avoided, all within the constraints of an economy that still relies too heavily on dirty fossil fuels."

In other words, it's a fallen world. But Al Gore is a good person, much better than most other people. And in any case, he's spent a lot on indulgences.

Skeptics continued to raise the same persistent question, and not just about Al Gore, but about countless elite environmental activists like Gore: If you really believed that the future of the planet was imperiled by carbon emissions, why would you fly private?

But this is missing the point entirely. Gore and DiCaprio and Hillary Clinton and the rest feel fine about flying on private planes not because they're hypocrites, but because they're entirely sincere. They care deeply about carbon emissions, much more deeply than you do. Caring deeply is the only measure that matters. That's why their consciences remain untroubled, no matter how many times they violate the standards they demand of others.

Once you understand this, the Paris climate accord makes sense. An international agreement designed to curb carbon emissions, negotiated next to Europe's busiest private airport. Nobody in attendance flew commercial. Nobody seemed to feel bad about it, either.

If you can take a private jet to a global warming summit without guilt, you're probably not going to be troubled by a few inaccurate predictions, even if those predictions formed the basis of flawed public policy that affected the lives of billions. Climate change activists give themselves permission to make mistakes.

It turns out that predicting changes to climate over time is more difficult than anyone suspected. Indeed it's never been done. A 2013 report by the Intergovernmental Panel on Climate Change found that over a twenty-year period, global temperatures hadn't risen nearly to the degree that models had predicted. In some cases, the predictions were so far off that the actual, observed temperatures fell outside their margin of error.

Keep in mind that these were sober predictions made by respected scientists using the best available data. They were still wrong. Lesser authorities have been even further off base.

In 1989, officials at the United Nations predicted that entire countries would be annihilated if warming trends weren't reversed by 2000. In 2007, the UN's former head of the IPCC predicted that if "there's no action before 2012, that's too late."

In 2008, ABC's *Good Morning America* estimated that, because of climate change, New York City would be underwater, "hundreds of miles" of the country would be on fire, and a billion people would be "malnourished" by 2015. By June 2015, ABC said with confidence that a carton of milk would cost $12.99 and a gallon of gas would be $9. "That's seven years from now," said anchor Chris Cuomo. "Could it really be that bad?"

As it turned out, no. But that didn't prevent the head of NASA's Goddard Research Center from predicting in 2009 that Barack Obama had "four years to save Earth."

Also in 2009, the head of Canada's Green Party said the world had just "hours" to "avert a slow-motion tsunami that could destroy civilization as we know it." Prince Charles of Great Britain estimated the West had just ninety-six months to save the planet. British prime minister Gordon Brown gave the rest of us "just 50 days to save the world from global warming."

By 2014, the foreign minister of France had extended that timetable. We have, he said, five hundred days to avert "climate chaos."

Clearly there's still a lot we don't know about climate change. To be fair, there's still a lot we don't know about a lot of things. After more than one hundred years of research, scientists haven't figured out what much of the human brain does. Researchers can't agree on the evolutionary purpose of sleep. These are basic questions, yet they remain shrouded in mystery. This is why hubris is the enemy of accurate conclusions. The minute you imagine a scientific debate has been settled, you start predicting nine-dollar gasoline.

Legitimate research requires relentless skepticism, a humility about conclusions, and a willingness to examine preconceived assumptions. Science isn't a scroll of revealed knowledge, or a discrete body of approved facts. It's a process by which we can gradually, incrementally understand how the world works.

A brilliant 2016 essay by William Wilson in *First Things* catalogues just how wrong much of what we think we know can turn out to be. Wilson cites a 2015 study by the Open Science Collection that did something never before attempted: researchers re-created one hundred peer-reviewed psychology studies in the field's three most prestigious journals to see whether their results could be replicated. The findings were grim: 65 percent of studies failed to replicate. Of those that did, many had far less conclusive results when they were re-created.

Psychology is a soft science at best, pseudoscience at worst, so Wilson pushed deeper. How did the hard sciences hold up to scrutiny?

Not well. Pharmaceutical companies now assume that about half of all academic biomedical research is false. Wilson cites one experiment in which scientists at the drug company Bayer attempted to replicate sixty-seven drug discovery studies that had appeared in top journals like *Science* and *Nature*. Bayer's scientists were unable to replicate the published results three-quarters of the time.

This doesn't mean that all scientific research is bogus. It

does mean that, no matter how many times Leonardo DiCaprio claims otherwise, science is never settled. Science is a practice, not a product.

This is no longer widely recognized. Roger Pielke is a tenured professor at the University of Colorado–Boulder. Among other things, Pielke studies the political uses of science. His own views on climate change are fairly conventional. Pielke accepts that global temperatures are rising, and has said that he is "personally convinced that it makes sense to take action to limit greenhouse gas emissions."

Pielke's mistake was in questioning the assumption that global warming has caused a major increase in extreme weather events, like hurricanes. Pielke published a piece suggesting that the rising cost of natural disasters might be driven primarily by economic growth, rather than climate change. There's more infrastructure than there was one hundred years ago, so the costs are higher when it's destroyed. It's an interesting theory. It turned out to be an unacceptable deviation from what all decent people know to be true. Pielke was punished for saying it.

Climate activists started a campaign to force Pielke from his side job freelancing for the statistics website FiveThirtyEight. After a few months, they succeeded. But the attacks on Pielke didn't end there. In 2015, Congressman Raul Grijalva of Arizona demanded that the University of Colorado turn over to Congress all of Pielke's private communications about climate change. The university refused, but Pielke learned his lesson. He stopped talking about climate.

Within academia, the pressure to conform to climate orthodoxy has rendered the scientific method irrelevant. Judith Curry, a longtime climatologist at Georgia Tech, resigned from her tenured position because of what she described as "craziness in the field of climate science." Over the course of her career, Curry has published two books and 186 articles on climate. But by 2016, the field was so politically fraught that academic journals refused to publish research that deviated from conventional opinion.

In an essay announcing her resignation, Curry wrote that "research and other professional activities are professionally rewarded only if they are channeled in certain directions approved by a politicized academic establishment." Discouraged by the stifling conformity, Curry gave up on academic journals altogether. She now publishes her research online. When science no longer requires evidence and no longer tolerates scrutiny, it's no longer science. It's dogma.

Bill Nye the Science Guy thrives in a world like this. A former stand-up comedian with a degree in mechanical engineering, Nye hosted a children's science show on PBS during the mid-1990s. The show went off the air and Nye faded into obscurity for a time. Thanks to elite concerns about climate change, he's back and more famous than ever. Nye's unrelenting alarmism resurrected his career.

Nye has no background in climate research, or in any of the natural sciences. He doesn't need one. When your job is to confirm the preexisting biases of people making more than one hundred thousand dollars a year, facts only get in the way.

When tornadoes hit Kentucky in the spring of 2016, Nye knew exactly what to say. "More severe weather. More suffering. More expense," he tweeted. "Let's all take climate change seriously."

When a storm hit Texas and wildfires broke out in Alaska, Nye blamed "global warming & climate change." According to

Nye, who disseminates most of his scientific opinions on Twitter, global warming is the cause of rainstorms in Texas, flooding in Louisiana and California, and an early spring snowstorm in the Northeast. For the consistency of his views, *Vanity Fair* declared Nye "the Face of Climate Change."

Nye takes the job seriously. When terrorists attacked Paris in 2015, Nye did his best to explain how climate change was at fault. Rising temperatures are a "very reasonable" explanation for Islamic extremism, Nye told the *Huffington Post*. Thanks to a drought in Syria, he explained, "there's not enough work for everybody, so the disaffected youths are more easily engaged and more easily recruited by terrorist organizations, and then they end up part way around the world in Paris shooting people."

The beauty of opinions like this is they're fundamentally impossible to disprove or rebut, though Nye has done his best to shut down any attempts. Questioning any part of climate orthodoxy, Nye has explained, is tantamount to "denying science" and is both "unpatriotic" and "unconstitutional." In one interview, Nye suggested jailing doubters who disagree with his views on climate change.

Some people look at statements like this and see echoes of the Soviet pseudoscience of the 1930s, where political orthodoxy determined the boundaries of acceptable research and resulted in generations of preventable failures. People starved to death because scientists were prohibited from telling scientific truths.

Others listen to Bill Nye and find themselves deeply impressed. On Earth Day 2015, then-president Obama made a video about climate change. In order to add scientific credibility, he invited Bill Nye to the White House to appear in it with him.

Increasingly, there are two kinds of environmentalists. I

sometimes think about that when I go fishing on the Potomac in Washington. I'm usually the only American-born fisherman on the river, and always the only one with a fly rod. Everyone else is from Mexico or Central America. They're using bait and fishing for food. They're always friendly. We nod as we pass on the path.

The river has changed over the years I've been fishing on it. It's still pretty but no longer tidy. There's now trash everywhere along the banks, beer bottles and takeout chicken boxes and soiled diapers. The homeless have left their rusting shopping carts and moldering sleeping bags. This section of the Potomac is on federal land, so the National Park Service has jurisdiction over it. You see park rangers driving by in their green trucks. I often wonder why they don't clean up the mess.

Then I remember: our environmental leaders don't care about litter anymore, or even about the state of the natural world, the birds or the riverbanks. They've got bigger concerns now—global concerns, moral concerns—that ordinary fishermen stepping over dirty diapers and Tecate bottles couldn't possibly understand or appreciate. But they feel good about themselves, and that's what matters.

EPILOGUE

Righting the Ship

Nothing that is happening in America today is unprecedented, or even unusual. A relatively small number of people make the overwhelming majority of significant cultural and economic decisions. Wars are fought, populations shift, the rules of commerce change, all without reference to what the bulk of the population thinks or wants.

This isn't strange. It's the story of all human history. Very few civilizations have operated in any other way. People naturally sort themselves into hierarchies. Those who have power defend it from those who don't. Rulers rule, serfs obey. It's a familiar system. We know it works, because it has for thousands of years.

The new ingredient, what makes our current moment so unstable, is democracy. Massive inequality can't be sustained in societies where everyone can vote. In order to survive, democracies must remain egalitarian. When all the spoils seem to flow upward, the majority will revolt in protest. Voters will become vengeful and reckless. They will elect politicians like Donald Trump as a sign of displeasure. If they continue to feel ignored, they will support increasingly radical leaders, who over time will destroy the ruling class, along with everything that made it prosperous. Left untended, democracies self-destruct.

There are two ways to end this cycle. The quickest is to suspend democracy. There are justifications for this. If your voters can't reach responsible conclusions, you can't let them vote. You don't give suffrage to irrational populations, for the same reason you wouldn't give firearms to toddlers: they're not ready for the responsibility. Nobody believes Jordan would become a happier country with free and fair elections.

But there's a cost to ending the vote. You can't install an autocracy without widespread repression and bloodshed, especially in a secular society. Saudi Arabia doesn't have revolutions because most Saudis accept that their royal family was installed by God. Nobody in East Germany ever believed that about their government. That's why the East German regime needed machine guns and a wall to keep its citizens from fleeing. There's no transitioning from democracy in America without civil war.

The other solution to the crisis is simpler: *attend to the population.*

Think about what they want.

If they start dying younger or killing themselves in large numbers, figure out why. Care about them.

If the majority is worried about something, listen. Give them back some of their power.

If they have strong feelings about an issue, don't overrule them, even if (maybe especially if) their views seem reactionary.

You can't force enlightenment by fiat. In a democracy, you can only persuade.

Go slowly. It isn't easy to relinquish control to people you have power over.

But try.

If you want to save democracy, you've got to practice it.

ACKNOWLEDGMENTS

The ideas in this book came from a lot of places, but they've been honed by the daily exchanges I've maintained for almost twenty-five years with my genius friend, Matt Labash; conversations I've had since 1987 with my college roommate and business partner, Neil Patel; near-continuous texting with my wise and hilarious brother, Buckley; and spirited weekly lunches with my father and hero, Richard Carlson. I'm grateful as always to the four of them.

Research for this book came from Blake Neff, Charles Couger, and Alex Pfeiffer, all of whom work on and greatly improve our nightly show on Fox. Pfeiffer, a fellow Grateful Dead fan, suggested the title.

Matt Latimer and Keith Urbahn from Javelin pushed me to write this book, and I'm glad they did. They give agents a good name. Jonathan Karp and Mitchell Ivers from Simon & Schuster made it possible.

Emily Lynn brought order and calm to the project, as she

does to everything. My executive producer, Justin Wells, solved every problem that stood in the way of writing a book and hosting a show simultaneously.

During the unpleasant moments, I drew inspiration from my spaniels, Meg and Dave. Their cheerfully single-minded focus on squirrels reminded me that complexity is usually the enemy of contentment.

Finally, nothing would be worth doing without my family: Susie, Lillie, Buckley, Hopie, and Dorothy. My deepest gratitude to them for a happy life.